SIX- FIGURE CHICKS

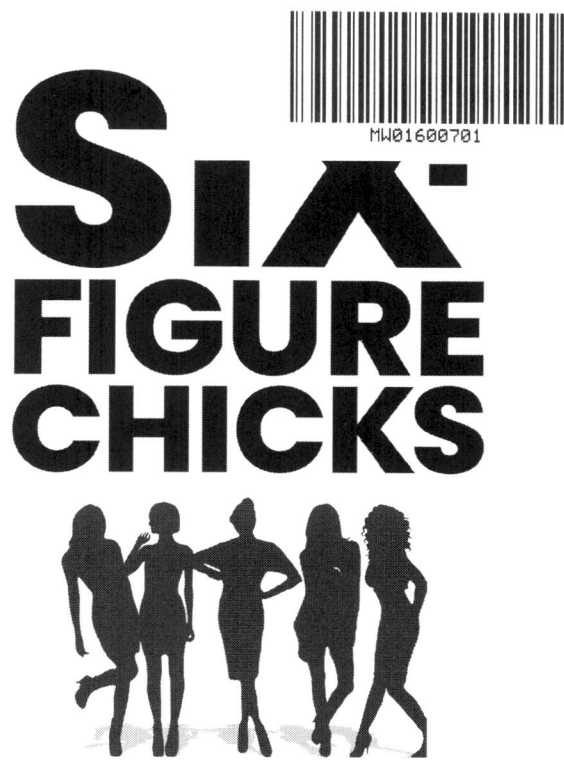

Compiled by

Mel Carr

CEO and Founder of Cloversy.com,
an Executive Virtual Assistant Company

Jumpstart
PUBLISHING

Published by K. Sawa Marketing International Inc. DBA Jumpstart Publishing. PO Box 6, Roseville, CA 95661. (916) 872-4000 www.JumpstartPublishing.net.

DISCLAIMER AND/OR LEGAL NOTICES

While all attempts have been made to verify information provided in this book and its ancillary materials, neither the author nor the publisher assume any responsibility for errors, inaccuracies, or omissions and are not responsible for any financial loss by customer in any manner. Any slights of people or organizations are unintentional. If advice concerning legal, financial, accounting, or related matters is needed, the services of a qualified professional should be sought. This book and its associated ancillary materials, including verbal and written training, is not intended for use as a source of legal, financial, or accounting advice. You should be aware of the various laws governing business transactions or other business practices in your particular geographical location.

EARNINGS & INCOME DISCLAIMER

With respect to the reliability, accuracy, timeliness, usefulness, adequacy, completeness, and/or suitability of information provided in this book, Cloversy, LLC and K. Sawa Marketing Int'l Inc. make no warranties, guarantees, representations, or claims of any kind. Readers' results will vary depending on a number of factors. Any and all claims or representations as to income earnings are not to be considered as average earnings. Testimonials are not representative. This book and all products and services are for educational and informational purposes only. Use caution and seek the advice of qualified professionals. Check with your accountant, attorney, or professional advisor before acting on this or any information. Earnings potential is entirely dependent on the efforts, skills, and application of the individual person.

Any examples, stories, reference, or case studies are for illustrative purposes only and should not be interpreted as testimonies and/or examples of what reader and/or consumers can generally expect from the information. Any statements, strategies, concepts, techniques, exercises, and ideas in the information and materials offered are simply opinion or experience, and thus should not be misinterpreted as promises, typical results, or guarantees (expressed or implied). This book is provided "as is," and without warranties.

ISBN: 979-8-9871985-0-6

Printed in the United States of America

Dedication

Special Thanks to:

Six-Figure Chicks is dedicated to all the impactful and successful women in my life, starting with my own grandmother, Alice. I would give anything to sit down with her and style her hair for hours.

My mother, Debbie, is the strongest woman I know. Thank you for always picking me up, no matter how many times I fall.

And last but not least, Anjanette—you are the sister I wish I had. You've always been there for me, even when I forgot to be there for myself.

Six-Figure Chicks is for all of us: for the women who have been told we're not good enough, smart enough, or pretty enough. Six-Figure Chicks is a reminder that we are all those things, and so much more. Thank you for being a part of this movement. Together, we will change the world.

Table of Contents

SECTION 3

I saw that six-figure women have two specific types of support that underearners seemed to lack—True Believers, people who recognize their potential and offer encouragement, and Way Showers, people who provide the map and serve as proof that success is possible.

- BARBARA STANNY,
Secrets of Six-Figure Women

Introduction

Six-Figure Chicks is a book that will inspire and motivate you to achieve more success than you can imagine!

What do we mean by "Six-Figure Chicks," exactly?

Yep, you guessed it...we make $100,000 OR MORE every year as business owners or in our careers.

Why did we create a book about good habits and stories from women earning six figures or more?

Because isn't that what everyone wants?

Well, it may or may not be what you think you want now, but it's absolutely possible!

And we're not talking about working our tails off while earning this income, either. While some of us DID do just that along the way, we eventually figured out how to do it without killing ourselves.

The goal of this book is to show you how to make a six-figure income (or more!) without killing yourself in the process—because NO ONE wants that.

Unfortunately, many women think that's what's required for financial success. Maybe you grew up with the mindset that in order to make more money, you have to work harder or put in longer hours at what you do.

The women who share their stories and strategies in this book are proof that it is possible to achieve great things, no matter where you come from or what your circumstances may be—and no matter what mindset you grew up with.

These women have all agreed to be a part of this book with me to "lift as we climb," bringing other women up with us. They are all hyper-focused on women achieving more, with more confidence and self-assurance than ever. We all want you to build a six-figure career or business with more ease, grace, and balance. YES, it IS possible to do that!

And who am I, and why did I come up with this concept?

When I was younger, I always looked up to the women who were successful in business. I admired their power and strength, and I wanted to be just like them. However, I wasn't sure how to get there. I didn't know what steps to take or where to begin. But then I realized that the key is just to start somewhere. It doesn't matter where you are or what you're doing. If you have a dream, go after it. Don't let anything stand in your way. And don't be afraid to fail. Every successful person has failed at least once, but they didn't let that stop them. They got back up and they kept going until they reached their goal. So, if you want to be a successful woman in business, just start somewhere and don't give up. The sky is the limit.

My name is Mel Carr and I'm the owner of a highly successful Virtual Assistant business called Cloversy at www.Cloversy.com. We help high-achieving women get the stuff done in their businesses that they aren't fond of, don't like to do, or just aren't good at. Women who know and play to their strengths also know their weaknesses, and they outsource those things. If you're ready to play a bigger game in your business and want help getting organized, outsourced, and systematized, then reach out and let's talk!

The Six-Figure Chicks in this book have all achieved a great deal of success in their respective fields, some in their previous corporate lives, and all as current business owners. We want to share our secrets and best practices along with how we overcame obstacles and challenges along the way. As you read our stories, we hope you will be inspired by our courage and tenacity. You will also gain insight into what it takes to create a higher income-earning and more successful career or business for yourself.

We are women who have defied the odds to become leaders in our fields. We've learned valuable lessons about what it takes to be successful in business, and we want to impart that wisdom to you so you can avoid our mistakes and act on our advice. We come from diverse backgrounds and industries, but we all have one thing in common: we are all six-figure chicks. In addition to sharing our "How we got here" stories, we're going to share tips on how we overcame the obstacles, challenges, and roadblocks. Then we'll offer advice on topics such as goal setting, networking, finance, spirituality, marketing, and work/life balance so that you can develop new, productive habits for running your business or career. This will help you move faster to your goals.

Whether you're just starting out in your career or you're already well on your way to success, there's something in this book for you. If you're ready to take your life and career to the next level, this book is for you.

The stories and advice from these six-figure chicks will inspire and empower you to achieve your dreams.

What are you waiting for? Start reading and get ready to be motivated!

Section 1

Our Stories, How We Got Here, and How to Connect with Us

In the first part of this book, you will get to read each author's story on how they got where they are now—in business, in their careers—and how they made it to Six-Figure Chick status. It's an introduction to the authors and their stories, how they grew their businesses and made it to six figures, so you can get to know them on a deeper level.

Alexandria Manning's
Story

If a picture is worth a thousand words, then what is your home saying about you? More importantly, what is your home saying about you—to you? Is it empowering you to step into self-love and confidence every day, or diminishing your ability to live the life you desire?

My name is Alexandria Manning, owner of Come Alive Interior Design. I am an Intuitive Interior Designer, Professional Home Stager, and Luxury Rental and Hospitality Consultant. Through my unique process, I help my clients discover the Interior Design elements they need to Come Alive in their homes. This process lays the foundation for every space I design. Once I know what elements empower you, I'm able to start a design concept from scratch, one that creates flow and maximizes storage for ease of use, and which reflects the vibrancy of the person using it. When you walk around your home it should be telling your story and helping you feel the transformative power of that story.

It seems we are constantly surrounded by the idea that we are either this thing or that, when in reality, we are all of the things. People are all beautiful puzzles! Of course, the part of you that thrives in your kitchen is going to feel and look slightly different from you in your living room, office, or bedroom. I've learned that there is no one-size-fits-all for how a space is created. I don't follow a system that gives me the same result for every situation, because my clients are all unique. Instead, I follow a process that allows me flexibility to create with and for you.

I was born in California and raised in Michigan and Oklahoma by two loving parents, and I have an older brother. As a child, I loved to express myself through creative ways. Starting when I was 4 years old, my older brother would come home from school, excited about things he was learning—and share them with me. I was taught to write my own name, and I was so excited about what I'd learned that I practiced anywhere I could find a surface, even on the door frames! My parents bought me an easel to prevent more creative expression on the walls, and my love of art and creativity solidified. I was hooked!

In college I majored in art, then photography. I was searching for what made me happy, brought out my gifts, and included enough diversity that my spontaneous personality wouldn't get bored with it. I loved trying new things and held a variety of jobs from State Park attendant to ranch work and tour guide.

After my first child was born, things shifted. I loved being a mom and my son was a miracle, having lived against drastic odds that had him on full life support at just 11 days old. When he finally came home 3 months later, I couldn't shake a guilty feeling that I wanted more. I was so grateful for him, and yet I felt like I was losing myself. I knew I didn't want to leave the home and have someone else raise my child, but what could I do? Multiple opportunities came into my life over the following 13 years which gave me valuable experience but very little income. Design was something I started doing as a release from the frustrations I was experiencing while trying to build a home-based career and life-sustaining income. When I designed, I was liberated from the confining reality around me and elevated into a realm where the only limits were the scope of my imagination. Then in 2019, a unique opportunity came for me to attend a business training, the kind to which you must be invited. Attending that event showed me the answers I'd been looking for were already right in front of me—and had been for years! I left that event with a registered business: Come Alive Interior Design was born.

Since its opening, Come Alive Interior Design has become more than just an Interior Design studio. Its services have grown to include professional Home Staging, Vacation Rental Design, and Hospitality Consulting. With the growth of the business, my husband has been able to step away from his full-time job as project controls manager for a major corporation and now uses those skills to serve our clientele as a licensed General Contractor. His knowledge and hands-on experience in the construction industry and in managing large projects and virtual drawings has been invaluable! With every new client our capacity expands. We continue honing our skills, developing new ideas to increase value, elevating client experience, and developing unique, tailored designs. It's also a dream come true for us to finally be working together to create the life we've been talking about for years.

Interior Design affects every area of our lives because it affects what we believe, think, and feel about ourselves—and that is incredibly powerful! I love working with my clients and getting to know them as we create an environment that empowers them to embrace who they are and to give more of their love and talents to those around them.

Favorite Quote

"Our deepest fear is not that we are inadequate. Our deepest fear is that we are powerful beyond measure. It is our light, not our darkness that most frightens us. We ask ourselves, who am I to be brilliant, gorgeous, talented, fabulous? Who are you not to be? You are a child of God. Your playing small does not serve the world. There is nothing enlightened about shrinking so that other people won't feel insecure around you. We are all meant to shine, as children do. We were born to make manifest the glory of God that is within us. It's not in some of us, it's in everyone. And as we let our own light shine, we unconsciously give other people permission to do the same. As we are liberated from our own fear, our presence automatically liberates others."

- MARIANNE WILLIAMSON

Recommended Affirmation

I AM ENOUGH. Break this down to "I AM," who is God, and it says "God is enough." All things are possible with God!

Alexandria's Special Offer

Thank you for reading my story! I hope it inspires and lifts you as you journey on to reach your goals! To help you as you move forward, I'd like to offer you a Free Guide to understanding the Interior Design elements that empower your inner self to COME ALIVE! Please go to www.SixFigureAlexandria.com for that gift!

About Alexandria Manning,

Owner and Creator of Come Alive Interior Design

Alexandria is an Intuitive Interior Designer, professional Home Stager, and Luxury Rental Design and Hospitality Consultant. She helps her clients identify which Interior Design elements help them Come Alive, then uses those elements as the foundation of her design work. Alexandria has won the Best of Houzz award for outstanding Interior Design services every year since she has been in business. She has been married to her husband Michael for 17 years. They have 3 amazing kids and enjoy a rural lifestyle in Northern Utah.

Ashlee McKinnon's
Story

I've been empowering women in my community for the past 16 years. When I opened my first studio, my goal was to create a space where clients could come and feel safe, and leave feeling confident and beautiful. While struggling with polycystic ovaries, uterine cancer, infertility, ADHD and anxiety disorders, and my own body dysmorphia, I realized that, through all the chaos, the quickest pick-me-up was getting my hair done. I couldn't fix any of my health issues overnight; working out and dieting takes months of consistency to see or feel changes, and raising children and staying happily married never ends. But I could change my whole look and have a great talk session in one afternoon in the salon.

Because I am so passionate about uplifting others and I just love people, I found myself treating my skill set like a hobby, and I was doing lots of favors. When my children were little, I would allow friends and clients to come to my home during nap time and we'd do "kitchen hair." These circumstances led to friends and clients asking for discounts, since they weren't receiving the "full" salon experience.

And I allowed it.

I felt guilty charging for my product, my time, and the skills I'd spent thousands of dollars to cultivate. I let the mom guilt get to me because

I wasn't cleaning the house or cooking a homemade meal from scratch while the kids were sleeping. Worse, felt horrible if I wasn't done with my client when the kids woke up or my husband got home!

I completely lacked the gumption to set or enforce any kind of boundaries with my clients, my friends, or myself—and of course, I burnt myself out. I would lie in bed at night pleading with God to help me be better, because I kept thinking I wasn't a good enough mom, I didn't make enough money to justify being away from the family, and I wasn't skinny enough or healthy enough. I felt like I didn't have control over my life or the direction it was headed.

This spiral in my mental health made my physical health worse and took a heavy toll on my relationships with my family, friends, and husband. I would literally say to him, "I know the words coming out of my mouth are completely irrational and crazy, but I can't help that I feel this way. The feeling is real, even if the scenario that's creating the feeling isn't real."

That's when I knew I needed to seek help from a professional and do some inner healing. I needed to find clarity, create structure out of my chaos, and prioritize the relationships that were most important to me. I had to start with myself. I needed to like myself, even if no one else did.

After meeting with my doctors and figuring out a plan to regulate my health, my husband and I both did some in-depth personality tests. We listened to self-help books and started implementing new communication patterns within our home and the people we worked with every day. There's this great book, "The Positive Personalities Profiles," that breaks down the different personality types and traits that go along with each profile, and the groups of people you'd expect to encounter with those personalities. The book even gives specific phrases each personality uses, and the meaning behind each phrase—but also how the different groups interpret those words.

It was such a profoundly eye-opening exercise that I really dug in and got honest about my faults and flaws and the traits I love about myself. I'm still continually striving to improve and become the woman God planned for me to be, and the woman I want to see myself become.

This series of events re-ignited my love of learning, and the classes I took and continue to take have ranged from time management skills, networking, and how to feel sexy and divinely feminine at any stage of life, to specific courses on color and extensions, jewelry making, and emergency preparation classes.

I was asked to teach a small group of fellow hairstylists a technique class, and I rediscovered my passion behind the chair. I never took a break from working, but for the first time I started working on my business and not just in it. I hired a beauty business coach who helped me create systems in my business that would allow me to start to scale and grow in the direction I wanted. I took back control and stopped waiting for all the good thing to happen to me. These systems helped me automate a lot of the time-consuming tedious work, giving me the freedom to be present with my family when I was home. I got serious about the numbers and figured out exactly how much it was costing me to provide the services I was offering. I also aligned myself with companies I could work with, and I learned from their owners. Within 6 months, I went from generating $500 in a 12-hour day to earning $1000-$1500 per day! I hit my first year of six-figure revenue only 12 months after hiring a business coach.

After working in my 150-square-foot studio for 12 years and traveling as a branded and independent educator, the opportunity to move into a salon space presented itself. Being self-employed and in the beauty industry, I didn't qualify for any kind of bank loan, small business loan, or angel investors. So, I chose to double down and bet on myself. I risked everything; I paid cash from our savings and used our personal credit cards to do the renovations. I moved in during construction and started working just to cover all the costs. One year into my new lease, the pandemic hit—and that was the first year I brought home six figures.

Since opening the salon I've grown my team, coached fellow beauty bosses, partnered with bigger brands, manufactured my own styling tools and hair care accessories, and developed a line of personal hair extensions. I've also deepened my relationship with my husband and children, built respectable healthy boundaries, created a clearer road map for my life, and I love myself!

Favorite Quote

"Every darkness we touch is just a pathway to greater light."
- NATALIE NORTON

Recommended Affirmation

I am the hero of my own story, even if I'm the villain of someone else's.

Ashlee's Special Offer

You can learn more about Ashlee or connect with her online at www.EraSalonAZ.com.

About Ashlee McKinnon

Ashlee lives in Gilbert, Arizona with her husband, three children, and two fur babies. She's been beautifying the area's heads of hair with her expertise in blonding applications and natural-looking hair extensions. She coaches fellow industry members in better business practices and technical training.

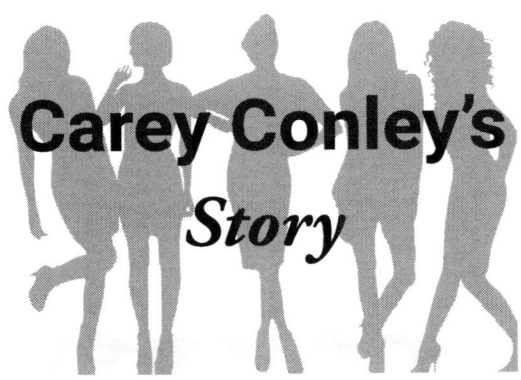

Carey Conley's
Story

Collaboration is one of my highest core values, which is why I feel so humbled and honored to be included in this book. It warms my heart and empowers me to be aligned with these other women who inspire me, and I hope my story will inspire YOU, too!

I grew up in a somewhat normal middle-class family in Denver, Colorado with two parents (who divorced when I was 29), and a younger brother. As a young girl I was strong-willed, imaginative, and bossy, and I longed to grow up to be a singer, a dancer, and an actress. My favorite thing to do was to play my records, sing into anything I could make into a microphone, and choreograph dance routines for me and my friends... my poor family!

My parents both worked, so overseeing my brother after school and during the summer months fell to me. I think it was because of this responsibility that I became very independent and determined at an early age. (This was NOT always a good thing!) I also started journaling the dreams I had for myself at age 14, and I always knew there was something special and unique that I was going to do in this world.

As most girls do at that age, I started listening and acting the way I perceived the world wanted me to be, just so I could fit in and be liked. I did the things that made me 'popular' instead of unique, and I remained like that for a very, very long time. To be transparent, I will tell you it has taken me until the past decade to not only become aware of my past habits, but to start letting all of that go. (As I write this, I am 60 years old.)

Tip #1: Be yourself, no matter what, and listen to your heart. God has a plan that is perfect for you, and YOU are the only one who can carry out that purpose!

I met my husband in high school, and after we both graduated with business degrees from Oklahoma State University, we moved back to Colorado to start our married life and professional careers. My husband was very successful in corporate sales. I, on the other hand, was changing jobs every two years until I finally realized that I did not fit the nine-to-five mold. With prompting from my first mentor, I decided to honestly look at what I wanted to be and do.

This was a watershed moment. It was not only a pivotal point for me, but the onset of what I would soon discover to be my life's work. I was encouraged to take a day off and, with a legal pad in hand, write out what I wanted my life to look like. I wrote several pages about the kind of woman I wanted to be as a person, a wife, a future mom, a leader in the community, and an entrepreneur so I could do what I was passionate about—plus make a difference. I now know something I did not know on that day, and I have since taught that "something" to thousands of people: I was listening to my own heart and discovering God's purpose for me. (This was about 1989, and I still have those pieces of paper.)

Tip #2: Write your own vision! Take a day, completely unplug, and for every area of your life (faith, family, friends, fitness/health, fun, finances, field/career), write out your heart's deepest desires in detail, as if you are currently three years into your future and your ideal life is actually happening. Leave NOTHING out, and don't worry about the 'how!'

One of my favorite quotes is, "Pencil in your plans. Write your vision in ink." What this means to me and you is that your vision is anchored in your purpose (which does not change), but the path to get there can change a lot. It certainly did for me.

A couple of years after writing my vision, we started our family. With a two-year-old son in tow and five months pregnant with our daughter, I finally took the leap: I quit my job to start my own business in the network marketing industry. It was everything I had envisioned, so I was all in! I worked very hard to build a team of leaders, earned all the trips and the car, and reached the top rank in the company. I achieved a LOT, but I must tell you, the journey was tough—mainly because of the painful personal growth I had to go through to become that leader. I see SO many women quit because they aren't willing to change themselves and, if needed, their environment. In addition, they often don't know where to start.

Tip #3: Have a vision so big it overrides the 'walls' you are facing, and each day, take three intentional steps toward that vision. Intentional and consistent daily goals are the key to reaching success in every area of your life!

Unbeknown to me, those 20+ years were preparing me for the bigger mission I am currently on, and for the tragic impacts that were coming. In 2012 I launched my speaking and coaching career, and for many years I had four mastermind groups that I coached. I have become known as the 'Vision Expert,' I have authored two books, and I continue to speak on stages worldwide. I am humbled to collaborate with some of the best thought leaders in the world.

It was shortly after launching this career that my husband of 30 years died by suicide, and three years later my son, at the age of 26, also died by suicide. I tell you this part of my story to make a major point, especially considering the world in which we currently live. NO ONE is exempt from trauma and the challenges of life, no matter what you see in the media. The great ones (like you!) are the ones who see beyond their current circumstances and ask, "How can I use this for good and be a light for others who are suffering?"

My last tip and request of you:

Today, despite all your fears and doubts, stop comparing and start doing anything you can to follow your own unique vision and purpose! I promise you, as you reach higher levels of yourself, those two elements of your life will always be there. If they are not, you are playing too small.

Today, for the sake of our future generations, I ask you to step all in for them. I am on a mission to change the trajectory of depression and suicide. The world needs you!

Favorite Quote

"The two most important days in your life are the day you were born and the day you find out why."

- MARK TWAIN

Recommended Affirmation:

I have everything I need in this very moment to create the life I desire!

Carey's Special Offer

Are you ready for more? Download your free copy of my "Vision is Victory" workbook today to begin working on what you truly desire and intend to create in your life. Go to www.SixFigureCarey.com now. This is the foundation for success!

About Carey Conley

Carey Conley is a coach who has helped hundreds of people around the country achieve success in their personal lives. Her story includes extraordinary moments, such as when she lost both husband and son to suicide 3 years apart. These experiences bring power to her message, which helps others find what they never thought possible for themselves. Carey has found her passion in helping men and women create visions so powerful, they propel their visionaries through life's challenges without hesitation or doubt, lifting each person toward greater heights!

Jen Du Plessis'
Story

Are your daily activities starting to feel a little like eating soup with a fork? Mine were, until I cracked the code to reaching uber-success in both my business and my life.

I was born in Colorado but raised in Michigan. I was an only child until I was 12, when my baby brother Sam came along. I was quite lonely as a little girl growing up in a household where my father was an alcoholic and my mother was a verbal abuser.

There was a tremendous amount of fighting in my household, but I was fortunate enough to live next-door to my grandparents and one of my uncles. They were a Godsend to me, and they still are to this day. They taught me so much about life and love.

My uncle is a jokester. He gave all the cousins nicknames. Unfortunately, my nickname was "Jenny who ain't got a penny." I didn't understand what he meant. So, I took it literally and put one in my shoe, so when he would say, "Hey there, Jenny who ain't got a penny," I would tell him, "No, I have one in my shoe!"

One day, I arrived home and walked in on another argument between my mom and dad. This was not a regular argument. My dad had a shotgun pointed at my mother's head. I ran out to my grandparents' house. I knew at that moment I would never allow myself to be in that position.

All of these difficult circumstances had me constantly seeking approval. I was going to prove to everyone that I would not become an alcoholic, a verbal abuser, or poor. I was determined to have more than one penny in my shoe; I would have millions.

In the tenth grade, I met the love of my life, a one-in-a-million. We were just like Danny and Sandy from the movie *Grease*. He taught me to do things that bring me love. He encouraged me to stop constantly proving my worth to others.

This mantra was easier said than done, because I had "people-pleaser" in my DNA. I did everything possible to prove my worth. I was runner-up in the Miss Colorado pageant, the state tennis champion, a soccer star, the only highschooler to play in the city's symphony, and a pre-med student. I was overachieving, but I was absolutely miserable inside. I just kept hoping that someone, anyone, would tell me they were proud of me.

I was proud of me, when I received my first salaried position making $120K as the VP of National Sales for a start-up dotcom company. I had made six figures several times prior, earning commissions in the mortgage industry, but this was different. This was a salary.

I entered the business sector in 1983 and, as most women do in the industry, I began as a receptionist/set-up clerk, on the operational side of the business. Men headed up the sales and management arenas. My parents never achieved this kind of success. Over the course of ten years, I moved up the operational ladder and into sales, earning the title of #1 Sales Rep in the country—but at what cost?

One day when I was out to dinner with my family, I stepped out of the restaurant to take a client phone call. I was walking back and forth on the "concrete balance beam" (pacing back and forth on the sidewalk). I am confident that you are familiar with that walk. I was telling the client, "I can help you with that, don't worry. I'm on it." Then, I happened to glance over into the window of the restaurant and saw my family breaking bread together, laughing, and making memories. It hit me: I was not part of those memories (or any others) while I was working. I was never mentally or physically present because my clients took precedence. I had vowed never to be absent like my parents, yet I was—just in a different way.

That moment changed my life. At that time, I was closing $50MM in mortgage loans annually, putting me in the top 1% of loan officers nationally. Not bad. The issue was, all the activities and hours I was putting in felt like eating soup with a fork. I was constantly busy, but never quite fulfilled.

I decided right then and there that I had to change the way I was doing business; I had to find a better way. If I could just figure out the code, I knew I would be able to make a significant change in all of our lives.

Three years later, I was able to crack the code by designing a system that attracted clients rather than having to chase after them. Soon I was saving time but achieving so much more.

Speaking of achieving, I received an award in recognition for being one of the top 200 loan officers in the country, out of a pool of 750,000. For the first time, I was being honored for my efforts. But I was so focused on becoming more efficient, I didn't even realize that I had closed $102MM in mortgage loans that year. It was just the start. I found myself in the seven-figure club, and I have remained there ever since.

Not long after I developed my proven system to work on purpose, attracting clients, hiring a power team, and working above my business, my husband and I took a one-month trip to Europe for our 30th wedding anniversary. This type of trip was unimaginable years earlier because of my workload. I could not have spared the time.

I took pause as my husband and I sat on the balcony of our bed and breakfast in Barcelona, Spain and thought about how blessed we were. I was finally able to live life to the fullest because we were financially secure, and because of the support of my amazing team, the business could run without me. That trip took away so much of the stress and anxiety that I had felt for many years.

I am done proving, and I am now living, finally making memories that matter.

Favorite Quote

"Do what is easy and your life will be hard. Do what is hard and your life will become easy."

-LES BROWN

Recommended Affirmation

Stop talking, take action, get results.

Jen's Special Offer

Looking for that magic bullet, the ONE thing that will make the difference? The answer is in this formula: Mindset + Methods = Momentum. If you are looking for a true breakthrough in your business and your life, grab my free gift online at www.SixFigureJen.com: The 7 Strategies to Breakthrough your Business Mindset.

About Jen Du Plessis

– America's Lifestyle Mastery Mentor

Jen has been in the financial services industry for 4 decades and was listed in the Top 200 of nationally ranked mortgage originators, having funded over $1 Billion in mortgage loans. As a 14X best-selling author, host of 2 podcasts and a TV show, she's an expert in Living a Life of Luxury, Priority and Time Management, Business Relationships, Scaling, and Sales. People most attracted to Jen are high-achieving professionals and entrepreneurs who are missing *something*. Through her masterminds, she helps people increase their awareness of what's possible to multiply their results in record time, while having the courage to say "yes" to their personal lives.

Jennifer Drago's
Story

I was born in New York to a salesman and his wife, who was once his secretary. My father passed away when I was three, so I was an only child with a single mother for my formative years. I spent most of my time by myself or with adults—listening and not interacting. I was highly intelligent, but embarrassed by my intelligence around my peers. I was painfully shy and had no friends. When I was nine my mom remarried, and we moved to Phoenix, Arizona.

On that move across the country, I decided that I would be a different person when I arrived in Phoenix. I made the conscious choice that I would no longer be shy, and instead I would "put myself out there." As I did so, I found that I was able to make lifelong friends, make the cheerleading squad, and get elected to the student council. It didn't come easily, and I still fight my introverted and shy tendencies to this day. This early experience shaped me and taught me that each day is a new opportunity to make a change for the better.

In high school and college, I worked for a serial entrepreneur, Tom, who recognized my skills and abilities early on. Over eight years, he gave me progressively responsible positions such as office manager and accountant for several companies. I was eventually asked to develop a new branch office in Seattle.

It was fairly unique for someone to entrust me with so much responsibility before the age of 21. I credit my self-confidence in business and my leadership skills to Tom. Interestingly, my mother and stepfather both owned small businesses during these years, but I gained my early business experience from someone outside of my own family.

I entered graduate school with an insane amount of real-life business experience that was unusual for someone of my age. I continued to work for Tom as I earned two master's degrees: one in health services administration, and one in business administration.

After grad school, I worked at the Arizona Hospital Association as the Director of Special Projects, where I oversaw a ballot initiative to increase the tobacco tax to fund indigent healthcare. After our first son John was born, I became a freelance consultant and worked from home, writing grants and business plans and facilitating a health coalition.

After that, I was hired as Director (and later became Vice President of Planning) at a hospital system with a strong nonprofit mission, two hospitals, and a full continuum of post-acute services. My responsibilities included strategic planning, facility planning, and new program planning. I planned two massive hospital expansions to serve the growing community, a new corporate center, and countless new programs. My proudest career moment was when I advocated for a new obstetrics program at our hospital, which was located in a retirement community. The service was needed because the neighboring community was comprised largely of young families. This program just celebrated its 20th anniversary, and has collectively birthed over 25,000 babies.

Speaking of babies, my second son Justin was born during my years in Planning, so I was experiencing the challenge of juggling a family and a busy career. Family always came first, and I was fortunate to work for leaders who felt the same.

I then became the Assistant Hospital Administrator for the two hospitals, where I oversaw 450 employees and had budgetary responsibility for $25 million. I oversaw several hospital departments and was responsible for preparing for visits from regulators and accrediting bodies. This was a demanding role, but one that I treasured because of the vast experience that it provided.

After 10 years in the hospital system, I launched an entrepreneurial venture which allowed me to spend more time with my sons during their adolescent years. I opened a franchised meal preparation business, which gave me great experience in streamlining operations and creatively marketing on a shoestring. I had the most successful franchise in the system, so I was asked to become a franchise consultant to help struggling franchisees. It was a brilliant concept with bad timing, because the economy hit a major recession after 18 months in the business. I had an exit strategy, and moved on quickly.

I spent a few fascinating years working part-time as a controller of several grocery warehouses, where I learned about the productivity and agile management that are necessary when margins are slim. The part-time role allowed me the flexibility to be present during my sons' teenage years, attend their games, participate in booster clubs, and serve as a team mom, activities that I would not have traded for anything.

Following that stint, I served as Vice President and eventually Chief Strategy Officer of a nonprofit senior living organization for 11 years. It was a rewarding job where I used my planning skills to identify unmet needs and develop wellness programs to serve the community.

I left my corporate position in 2021 and founded my own consulting company, Peak to Profit, to help service-based business leaders develop a laser-focused strategy to move their businesses forward by scaling, increasing profits, or amplifying their impact.

My sons are now in their twenties and building their careers. My husband and I will celebrate 30 years of marriage in 2023. My husband, John, is a talented Chief Financial Officer and high-school football coach, and he is my biggest supporter. He has made all of this possible by being my best friend and teammate.

I believe my career success was made possible by leaders who believed in me and gave me opportunities to manage huge projects, budgets, and teams in a manner that pushed me outside of my comfort zone. My husband and children were always my top priority, and I also had the good fortune of working for leaders who allowed me to have a work-life balance and prioritize my family in that way.

Favorite Quote

"Everything you want is on the other side of fear."
- JACK CANFIELD

Recommended Affirmation

"I don't chase, I attract. What is meant for me will find me."

Jennifer's Special Offer

Get free access to my on-demand course, "Align Your Impact: Build a Vision and Strategy to Guide Your Business Growth." This self-guided curriculum will help you develop the foundational vision, strategy, and goals in a repeatable framework that will provide daily clarity, focus, and confidence. Several bonuses are included, such as productivity secrets and scorecard templates. Visit the special page here to access your freebies: www.JenniferDrago.com/sixfigurechicks.

About Jennifer Drago
FACHE, MHSA, MBA

Jennifer Drago helps serviced-based entrepreneurs and business leaders develop and implement a laser-focused business strategy, so they increase profits and increase their impact.

For 30 years, Jennifer worked as a strategy and operations executive in nonprofit healthcare and senior living organizations, developing and implementing strategies and programs to guide their growth. In her career, she has launched more than 20 successful business lines, as well as three nonprofits. She has also been an entrepreneur several times over and knows firsthand how challenging it can be to work ON the business while also working IN the business every day.

Julie Jones'
Story

When I was asked to be part of this book, my initial thought was, "Who am I, and what do I have to contribute?" Honestly, that was my first fleeting thought before my enthusiastic "Hell yeah, I'd love to be part of the book!" Every day, just like you, I question what I have to offer the world. What is my value? What is my worth? Then, I take a look in the mirror and I remember who the f*&k I am: I am the one and only Julie Jones.

Well, it wasn't always like that. I was born Julie Rosolek into a middle-class Catholic family where I was the oldest. I have a younger brother, Joe, and it was the two of us who grew up in Wisconsin where we played outdoors until dark, went fishing on Lower Post Lake, fought in the backseat of the car on family road trips, and shared a love of comic books. My brother and I are close. Even though I am in Arizona and he lives in Wisconsin, we talk almost every day. We are even closer now that we are "orphans." Our mom passed away 18 years ago, and our dad passed away 3 years ago. We never hang up the phone without saying "I love you," because we've learned that we don't know if we will have another chance.

There are so many parts of my story that make me who I am today, it's hard to narrow down the most important ones. I was bullied in grade school and high school, which left me insecure around women.

In fact, it's one of the reasons why I went to a male-dominated college and I decided to become a police officer. I know now that the reason I decided to protect and serve was to prove that I was worthy and could be courageous in the face of danger. I never felt courageous when I was being bullied as a child. So often, I backed down. I felt ashamed, and so alone in the world. It's another reason why I believe in including everyone in my circle of friends and my tribe. As human beings, we are all having this experience called "life." It's better to do it together than to do it alone.

There are many instances in which my resilience and unshakable faith in my life allowed me to power through the worst experiences, and now I look back and I realize those events happened for me, not to me. I am in my third marriage. In my previous two marriages, I walked away with very little, determined to figure it out and begin anew. There has always been a fire in my belly to figure it out and persevere.

I have experienced success in many careers, yet they left me unfulfilled. As a police officer, I had a worthiness issue that I was attempting to prove. Then, I became a property manager, a chiropractic assistant, a makeup artist, I worked for a personal growth company, and I pursued several direct sales companies. Each of my jobs gave me the opportunity to figure myself out, to acknowledge that I am destined to help people in a bigger way. Yet, I knew deep in my heart that they were not the right fit. I have a strong work ethic, a desire to succeed, and a drive to make the world a better place. In each of the aforementioned positions, I would start strong with that fire in my belly, only to realize the fire was quickly extinguished because, with each job position, I had to answer to someone else. I was working for someone else's dream, not my own.

The pandemic hit in March 2020, just as I was ready to launch an in-person workshop. The ideas had been rolling around in my head. I knew where my passion and purpose were in life: I wanted to motivate people to live in the moment and stop waiting for tomorrow. I saw first-hand throughout my life that tomorrow is not promised. Even in my own life,

I was tired of letting fear stand in the way of truly living the life I knew I was capable of. With no marketing experience and no idea what the heck I was doing, I started with an idea to have an online workshop for 3 hours in April 2020. Let me tell you, 3 hours seems like an eternity when you are doing your first event. I had a wealth of information to share, and I wasn't sure whether anyone would attend. Did what I had to offer really matter? YES, IT DID! I had 27 people in attendance at the first workshop, and from that event, I secured my first 3 coaching clients. When I heard that first inquiry, "How can I work with you?", I felt my doubts and fears slip away for the first time, and I KNEW I was on the right path.

I officially launched The Adventures of Julie Jones, LLC, in November 2020, and let's just say it's been like Mr. Toad's Wild Ride. I have been featured on numerous summits, spoken on a virtual world stage with Les Brown, appeared in numerous publications, featured on a magazine cover, authored an international best-selling book, and in November 2022, I will be launching my own television show, *Stop Waiting, Start Living*, along with a two-day conference designed to take overworked and overwhelmed individuals to a life of ease and FUN!

Sometimes I look back on my life and I don't even recognize who I was 10 years ago. I marvel at who I have become, how I am living the life I only dared to dream about. So many people along the way believed in me, and they saw my greatness before I believed in myself. I am still a work in progress, on a never-ending journey, taking people along with me to show them that anything is possible if they just believe. I am not good at taking no for an answer, for I truly believe that there are an infinite number of possibilities just waiting for you to say "YES!"

Favorite Quote

"I'm having fun. I'm being myself. I'm doing what I love. That's all that matters."

- JAMES CHARLES

Recommended Affirmation

I am living my life with ease and fun.

Julie's Special Offer

Are you ready to boldly live out loud and get off the hamster wheel of life? Do you crave more fun and adventure in day-to-day living? If so, download my fun-filled guide on how to incorporate simple ideas that will bring more ease and joy to your life. I am also including a video that will help you to be more productive without losing your sanity. Check me out at www.SixFigureJulie.com.

About Julie Jones

Julie Jones is an Award-Winning Speaker, International Bestselling Author of the book *Stop Waiting, Start Living*, and an Adventure & Breakthrough Coach who is currently launching her own television series, *Stop Waiting, Start Living*. She is a master connector of people who is passionate about supporting high-achieving entrepreneurs in getting off the merry-go-round of feeling overworked, overwhelmed and tired. Julie focuses on being in the moment and living life easily, effortlessly, and with more fun! As a former police officer and SWAT member, Julie knows that there is no promise of tomorrow, and she coaches individuals to face their fears and take massive, inspired action.

Katrina Sawa's *Story*

I never thought about having a career or a business that made me over $100,000 per year; that wasn't a goal for me while I was growing up. My parents didn't make over six figures from their jobs, and I doubt my grandparents did either—although they did do very well for themselves. I never felt like we didn't have money; I was lucky in that way.

I went through college without knowing exactly what I would be when I "grew up." I got a business and marketing degree, and graduated while tending bar at a local Mexican restaurant–*my parents were so proud!*

I took a job doing door-to-door sales after college, which is where I met my "starter husband." Then I went on to work for Enterprise Rent-a-Car (ERAC), where I worked like a dog and made good money, but I didn't get past Assistant Manager for promotions. I just wasn't a good fit for that type of structure and responsibility. I never made it to six figures in that job, or in my next few jobs in marketing or sales either; it still just wasn't on my radar to achieve.

I was 32 when I finally launched my own business after telling my last boss to "Fuck off." He wasn't supportive at all, and he would say one thing and do another. I simply had it one day and walked out, not at all worried about burning that bridge: I was going to be my own boss!

Luckily, I was very good at sales, marketing, follow-up, and connecting with people in general. Looking back now and comparing myself to other entrepreneurs who weren't as skilled in those areas, I recognize that those skills were pivotal to my success.

One thing ERAC did teach me was that it paid to be a hard worker. The more overtime I worked, the more money I made. Doing door-to-door sales also trained me to do a certain amount of daily activity to make the money I wanted. In fact, the goal was always to knock on 100 doors a day; that way, I was usually guaranteed to make my desired 10 sales a day (which, by the way, made me only $100 per day).

When I sold advertising for the local newspaper back in 2000, I was number one in sales for my office because I had that mentality. I would call on a certain number of businesses each day, by phone or drop-by. I was more consultative than my associates; I was not just an "order taker" when I spoke to them. That brought me a very high 5-figure salary, plus bonuses.

So, when I decided to jump into entrepreneurialism, I figured there would be a certain amount of activity I would need to accomplish daily in order to be successful, and I was right. I used everything I'd learned to get to know and build relationships with as many people as possible.

I joined the Chamber of Commerce. In fact, I joined four different chambers in my area! I joined the local BNI Networking Group, and a local Women's Business Group. I was a massive action-taker and a huge networker! I learned to love networking; I became very well-known.

Networking and follow-up, along with a great attitude and the ability to sell my services, are what really helped me build up to a high 5-figure business within those first few years.

The problem was that the cash flow wasn't as consistent as I'd have liked—or as my then-husband liked, either). Three years into my business, a friend suggested I attend a workshop to learn how to do more online marketing and build up my revenue. I wanted to go, but my husband said we didn't have the money for me to do so ($3,000 for the workshop, plus the hotel, food, and airfare), and he was right.

I felt in my gut, however, that the workshop would truly help me figure out how to become more successful. I knew it would be just what I needed to build a more consistent moneymaking business. So, I moved money around from one credit card to the next, leveraging my credit to buy the ticket and get there. I figured it out, and went anyway.

That workshop opened my eyes to what else was possible!

I couldn't believe so many people were working with clients all over the country via phone! I also couldn't believe the amount of money some of them were charging, and getting, for what they were offering!

I went home and changed everything about my business. I hired the gal who had run the workshop to show me what I needed to do over the next year. I even joined her $15,000 mastermind!

As you can probably imagine, my husband wasn't happy about what I was doing. I didn't know how I was going to pay for it, either; I just trusted and had faith that it would all work out.

By the following year, I was making more money than ever. I was not quite at six figures yet, but I did see HOW I was going to make $100,000 a year and what I had to sell in order to get there. That was my new goal.

Within the next year, my husband and I split up; we simply didn't have the same goals anymore. I had grown so much over that last year, and I wanted a lot more for myself than I had before. I was learning a lot about entrepreneurialism and what it really took to become successful, which got me excited to do new things and invest in big ways. The risky ideas were just too much for him, and I didn't want to settle for being "comfortable." I needed and wanted more.

I went back to that same workshop five times in two-and-a-half years, and every time I went, I raised my rates and developed something new, and I continued to participate in that mastermind with my mentor for a second year.

The people who I met during that time, I still call friends to this day. Many of us are peers now, and collaborate in business. I ended up joining a second mastermind for $25,000 the following year with a man who claimed he would help me make more money. It turned out he was a mindset mentor who focused on the subconscious mind, and whose process was tough love to getting to the big money goals. That was the turning point for me in my business. I had been resistant to learning about and understanding the subconscious mind. I hated the exercises he suggested at his events and in our group retreats. I was very uncomfortable.

He and the group had confidence in me, but all that "self-growth" was painful for me to go through. My parents never really talked about their "feelings," and they didn't open up nearly as much as these people wanted me to. All year, I cried in our mastermind meetings and through my coaching calls, because they kept telling me that all I had to do to get to the six-figure mark was to "Be Love."

Be Love? What the heck do I DO to "Be Love?"

I wanted the action plan, the activities I needed to "DO," just like I'd had through all the years prior in my business and my jobs. What were those things I needed to DO every day/week so I could bring in more income?

Nope—all I got was, "Be Love!"

Frustrated beyond belief, I attended events, conferences, and networking meetings, and I simply tried to "BE." I would walk in, open my heart (as they suggested), and just feel my way through the room, intuitively seeking out who I was meant to sit next to or talk with. To my surprise, people started becoming very attracted to me, wanting my advice, wanting to talk to me and listen to me. They'd lean in more, hiring me as their coach.

Aside from the business networking, I had been single and dating for about three years, and I was really hoping to find a new love relationship. I longed for that love connection, but the people at these events weren't exactly who I was looking for. Little did I know that I was putting feelers out into the Universe to attract not only $100,000 in my business, but also a significant other.

And I couldn't believe it, but at the end of that year, I got it. I got it all–both the $100,000+ business AND the man who I suspected would become the love of my life! At the end of that year, I found LOVE and MONEY!

That was the beginning of my six-figure journey. Every year thereafter, I slowly but surely increased my revenues, and today (twenty years later) I'm in multiple six-figures. It's great, but it's nowhere near enough. I have found that, when you grow emotionally and financially, you want more: you want to do more, be more, give more, and have more. I increase my money goals a little more each year to stretch outside my comfort zone. I used to have a goal of earning 7 figures, but that's not my focus anymore. My goals now are to live a happy, healthy, love-filled life with my "Keeper Husband" and my stepdaughter, making more than enough money to sustain our amazing lifestyle.

Favorite Quote

"If you think you can, or you think you can't, you're right."
— HENRY FORD

Recommended Affirmation

I am worthy of being loved and supported 110% of the time.

Katrina's Special Offer

Get free trainings on multiple ways to jumpstart your business, marketing, sales, systems, website, book, speaking, and team—plus, I've gifted a video training just for those of you reading this book! Access this video, and soon you'll be on the fastest path to six figures! Go to www.SixFigureKat.com.

About Katrina Sawa

Katrina Sawa is the CEO and Founder of JumpstartYourBizNow.com and JumpstartPublishing.net. Known as The JumpStart Your Biz Coach, she kicks her clients into high gear so they can start making more money doing what they love—and fast. Katrina is the creator of the JumpStart Your Marketing & Sales System, 10x International Best-Selling Author with 18 books, including *Love Yourself Successful, Jumpstart Your New Business Now, and the Jumpstart Your _____ (blank) Series*. She's the Founder of the International Speaker Network, a free, educational networking group with thousands of members. She's been featured on the Oprah and Friends XMRadioNetwork, ABC, The LA Tribune, and TheCW.

Lauren Otto's
Story

If you had told me in college that I would own a thriving, multiple-six-figure (projected to hit seven figures this year!) business, I would have laughed you right out of the room. In fact, I probably would have chosen courses in almost any other subject before I would have chosen courses in business. Oh, how life twists and turns. It somehow always lands you right where you are supposed to be.

I originally wanted to become a nurse. I've always wanted to help people, and I knew nursing would provide me with a nice, steady job and a comfortable paycheck. After a mediocre performance in my coursework and outright failing my clinicals, I realized this particular career choice wasn't for me. I changed my major to psychology in the middle of my junior year.

That was in 2004. My fancy $100,000 private college bachelor's degree landed me a job as a medical receptionist and a waitress at a large chain restaurant. My solution to my inability to land a career-worthy job was to go to law school! I chose this path not because I wanted to be a lawyer, but because it was an extension of my liberal arts degree; I thought it would open more doors.

I took four-and-a-half years to finish so I would have time for more practical experiences to beef up my resume for next time around. By the time I was in my last semester in the fall of 2008, the financial collapse was in full swing, and Lehman Brothers went bankrupt. I was working at the Department of Human Services for the State of Minnesota with intentions of being a shoo-in for a job there upon graduation, but the financial turmoil put the State of Minnesota in a hiring freeze for the foreseeable future. By the time I passed the bar exam, there were 200 applicants for every attorney job opening in the Minneapolis/St. Paul area, and I was competing with newly-unemployed attorneys with 3-5 years of experience. My fancy $150,000 law license had landed me back at that same chain restaurant.

The well had obviously dried up in the Minneapolis/St. Paul area, so I started to look at other communities. My husband grew up about an hour away in Eau Claire, Wisconsin, a city of about 70,000, so I started looking there. I contacted a local attorney about employment prospects, and I was told that the area needed attorneys to take contract public defender cases. I could get started right away, billing out my time at $40 per hour. I never wanted to practice, but I also didn't want to be a waitress with my law license. So, I took another bar exam, my second in two years, and moved to Eau Claire, Wisconsin.

It looked like my fortunes were about to turn around when I was offered a job shortly after I arrived! The job was with a small family law firm in the area that was run by women who were getting close to retirement: a fantastic opportunity. Thinking I could now support a family, my husband and I decided to get started. I shared my happy news with my employer about five months into my employment. They were not happy.

While they verbally expressed their congratulations, everything changed around the office. They stopped including me in their office socials and began the process of pushing me out. They completed that process two months later, which left me jobless and six months pregnant. I had contract work as a prosecutor to get me by, but that ended shortly before my due date. I took two months off to give birth and recover, then started my own law firm with my two-month-old baby at my side.

Thankfully, I had a very accommodating daycare that let me drop my baby off for court and pick him up when I got done. They also let me pay when I got paid. Eventually, I started to get regular paychecks, and I got busy enough to enroll him full-time. After a while, I realized that my earning capacity was quite limited at $40 per hour because I could not afford any overhead. I wanted an office and, eventually, some staff; I had realized that I could make more money if I had someone to help me with the administrative work for which I could not bill.

I slowly started to learn how to grow and run a business. I learned how to market, and I learned the necessity of systems, processes, and procedures. My goal was to get private family law clients who would pay me $250 per hour so it would be easier to pay myself and my overhead. I quickly realized that I liked the "business end" of my law firm better than I liked serving my clients. Guess I should have taken advantage of those business course offerings in college!

My private family law client base grew as my marketing efforts started to pay off. I hired my first paralegal in 2013 and my second in 2015. I merged with another attorney's firm in 2016 and hired my first employee attorney in 2018. I bought my partner out of the business in 2019 when he retired. I now have two full-time employee attorneys, two paralegals, a legal assistant, and an office manager. I am no longer actively representing clients. Instead, I am focusing on growing my firm and setting my employees up for success. I have also created a trademarked mediation service called Divorce in a Day that has been very successful in my local area. My next step is to launch the service nationally, teaching the model to attorneys in other states and creating a national brand.

This is not the path I would have chosen for myself, but thank goodness the universe landed me here anyway. I am right where I belong, creating services and growing businesses with the goal of making a difference for couples and families, and for the attorneys who serve them, for generations to come.

Favorite Quote

"Feel the fear and do it anyway."
- SUSAN JEFFERS

Recommended Affirmation

I am amazing!

Lauren's Special Offer

Want to learn more about how I was able to change my business to make it more peaceful and profitable? Go to www.SixFigureLauren.com for a special offer on my book, *From Burnout to Bliss: My Journey to the Peaceful, Profitable Family Practice of My Dreams.*

About Lauren Otto

Lauren Otto is the author of *From Burnout to Bliss: My Journey to the Peaceful, Profitable Family Practice of My Dreams*, and the founder and owner of Otto & Steiner Law, SC in Eau Claire, Wisconsin. She started her business from her home in 2011 with her two-month-old baby next to her, and has grown her business to include seven employees, including two employee attorneys, and projects seven-figure gross revenues this year. She is also the creator of the Divorce in a Day service, a trademarked revolutionary divorce mediation service that saves cooperative divorcing couples time and money on their divorce, all while getting the professional advice they need to get through the process smoothly. She is in the process of introducing the concept to other attorneys worldwide in order to benefit as many people as possible.

Mel Carr's
Story

It was scary yet exciting when I went from zero to six-figure earnings in my first year of business. I had no goal of making that much money the first year; my only goal was to make enough money to survive. I moved to Phoenix, AZ, less than a year after living overseas for almost eight years. My circle of friends was small; I could count that total on one hand.

When I first moved to Arizona, I applied to several jobs with no luck. That was a frustrating time for me. I moved to a new city alone, with no job and just a few friends. What was I going to do if I didn't find work? I asked myself that a lot, and I often talked myself off the ledge of depression. It was a lonely time for me. However, I knew that I could not just give up and do nothing. I had to work, find a job, or find a way to make money.

I had been an entrepreneur before; I could do it again. In grade school, I'd sold gum packs marked up, and made stress balls from flour and balloons. The earnings from that company were nowhere near what my company brings in today. What a great memory that is, in any case. I have been ready for this exciting ride since I was a little girl.

So, I put on my big girl pants and started thinking about what kind of business I wanted to create. I began meeting new people in Phoenix, and naturally, the question of what I did would come up. How would I answer that question? I had just moved there, so saying I was an entrepreneur would open up a can of worms and bring on questions I didn't want to answer yet, such as what kind of business and how long have you been in business?

I decided to be honest and tell people I was looking for work and trying to start a business. Some people would look at me with pity, some with genuine excitement. Some people wanted to know more. I met one woman in particular who became my first client. She was excited about my story and decided to take a chance on me. That was the beginning of my business journey here in Phoenix.

I continued meeting new people and started building relationships. I had one big client who made up most of my revenue, and then they closed their business. Suddenly, I was in survival mode again. However, I had a few clients and a few more prospects. I was not starting from zero this time, which gave me peace of mind.

It was still an uneasy chapter in my entrepreneurial time because if one client closed their business, what would happen if others did the same thing? And that's precisely what happened: another client closed up shop. I realized that I could not just rely on a handful of clients; I needed more. How would I do that? Where would I find new clients? I had to expand my network.

Ah, network. The concept hit me like a massive slap in the face. Duh, Mel, you must leave your house and meet new people at networking events. I remembered them so well from my corporate days. They were a little different now, however. I was marketing myself and my business, not working for another company. Initially, I was a little apprehensive. But I knew I had to do it.

I went to my first networking event, and it was a blast! I met some fantastic people and potential clients, and gained new ideas for growing my business. One new idea, mainly, involved more networking: a networking group. That six weeks of in-person training taught me a lot about how to attract the right client, who my "right client" was—and it even gave me a new client.

My biggest gain from that networking session was my first business coach. She was amazing! Even though I did not always look forward to our meetings, I knew I had to make it each week. It wasn't that I didn't like her; she was simply holding me accountable for making goals and sticking to what I had set out to create: a successful business.

She asked me what my income goal was. I had never before been asked that question. I told her I wanted $100,000. And I soon hit my six-figure goal. Wow, I had made that amount within my first year of business! It was an exciting time, but I knew it was just the beginning. There is always room to grow and become better.

That first year in business is always the hardest, they say. I would have to agree. It was a rollercoaster of emotions and self-doubt. Would I make it? Where would my next client come from? How would I attract them? All these questions and more swirled around in my head most days (and they still do).

There were good days when new clients came on board or revenue was up from the month before. Those days kept me going and reminded me why I had become an entrepreneur in the first place: because I loved the challenge, the risk, and the reward.

The biggest lesson I learned during my first year in business was to never give up, no matter how hard it gets. When you feel like you can't go on, take a step back, breathe, and remember why you started in the first place. That is what will carry you through to the other side. And if you don't know why you started, find someone who will remind you—like a business coach!

Favorite Quote

"A successful business is one that earns more money than it spends. A successful entrepreneur is one who can figure out how to do that."

- MEL CARR

Recommended Affirmation

I am diligent, detail-oriented, and organized. I can handle any task that is thrown my way.

Mel's Special Offer

Learn more about Mel and watch a video about hiring a virtual assistant to help you grow and scale your business at www.SixFigureMel.com. While you're there, sign up for a Free Discovery Call to see what can truly be taken off your plate so that you can focus on what you do best.

About Mel Carr

Mel Carr is the owner of Cloversy, a US-based Executive Virtual Assistant company that supports entrepreneurs looking to scale their businesses. Mel has been working as an Executive Assistant for over ten years and has a wealth of experience in helping business owners manage their time and priorities. Cloversy was created with the goal of providing high-quality support to entrepreneurs who want to grow their businesses without sacrificing their time or energy. Mel is passionate about helping business owners achieve their goals and provides her clients with the highest level of service possible.

Shari Weller's
Story

I grew up in the traditional American family where I was taught to go to school, get an education, find a career, and be loyal to my employer. Boy, things have changed since then!

Even though I am very grateful for a successful 15-year career in Corporate America, I am more grateful for taking the road less traveled to become an entrepreneur. While climbing the corporate ladder was fun for a while, the view from the top was not all that it was hyped to be. In reality, it was lonely and stressful. As a woman in a male-dominated field, I was always trying to prove myself, and even though my responsibilities were greater than those of most of the men with whom I worked, I was paid just a fraction of what they were paid. It wasn't until I had a health crisis after my first son was born that I finally took a step back to re-evaluate my priorities and values.

I knew I wanted to put my family first and stay at home, but I also wanted to contribute financially. Family is one of my core values, so I made the smart business decision to retire from corporate and devote myself to being present while raising a family. I knew I didn't want to miss out on any milestones.

Starting a network marketing business just made smart business sense. I researched home-based businesses, and I soon realized that network marketing was the vehicle that would give me the freedom and flexibility I desired, while allowing me to serve others and contribute financially to our family.

With a new lease on life and a strong sense of purpose, I quickly replaced (and surpassed!) my full-time income working part-time. I was determined to not only help my family, but to help other families as well. I knew there were other women who wanted to be home with their kids, and I knew there were other women who were burnt out with the grind of Corporate America. I had the best of both worlds! I was able to be a stay-at-home mom to my boys, the kind of mom I wanted to be. But I was also an entrepreneur, showing my boys how to build a business and leading by example. While the perks of being a business owner are many, the biggest blessing to me was for my boys to be able to watch their mom grow in a leadership role and help others achieve their goals.

While raising my boys and building my business, I developed a strong passion for helping people build businesses—and also for helping people with their health. I became a student of nutrition and grew passionate about taking a holistic approach to wellness. The more I learned, the more I wanted to share with others and make a difference in families' lives from a health perspective. I firmly believe your true wealth is in your health. I am committed to living a healthy lifestyle and to setting the example not only for my family, but for other families as well.

I thought I would always stay with my company and never considered changing; however, after 17 years of building a business with the same company, I decided to start over with a new company! I gave up a 17-year business with a residual income to start over. Once again, I chose to follow my passions and keep true to my core values. Once I saw what my current company was doing to not only disrupt the wellness industry, but the network marketing industry as well, I knew I had to be a part of it! Change is always scary, but it is what grows and stretches us. I knew if I could make a six-figure income once, I could do it again.

I am determined to impact as many lives as possible through this incredible opportunity, but also through a product line that can provide so many health benefits.

Favorite Quote

"SUCCESS is when I add value to MYSELF; SIGNIFICANCE is when I add value to OTHERS"

- JOHN MAXWELL

Recommended Affirmation

"I am grateful for all the abundance in my life."

Shari's Special Offer

Get your FREE eBook today and discover how to «Gain the Financial Freedom to Happily Kiss Corporate Goodbye!»
Go to: www.ShariWeller.com/partnerwithme

About Shari Weller

Shari is a proud wife, mom, entrepreneur, and a top 1% network marketing leader. Shari spent 15 years in Corporate America before finding her purpose as a mom and an entrepreneur. Shari is a fitness and nutrition enthusiast and loves networking. She has a heart for helping and mentoring people in business. She is a certified leadership and wellness coach, a philanthropist, and co-host of the Kiss Corporate Goodbye podcast.

Yancey Taylor's
Story

I am a firm believer in divine timing and that everything is exactly as it should be. Everything that has happened in my life has led me to the exact place where I am today, all in perfect timing. What's meant to be will always be, and I truly feel like my story is a perfect example of this. Our trials and tribulations, as difficult and challenging as they may be, all serve their own purpose to get us to where we are truly supposed to be.

In my twenties, I lived a very exciting life full of interesting decisions and lots of adventure. I lived in Los Angeles, California for most of these years. I loved being outdoors, going on hikes, sunbathing at the beach, riding my beach cruiser, and traveling to tropical destinations. Those were the days! At the age of twenty-six, I started noticing the effects of all the years of cumulative sun damage on my skin. I was dealing with major sun damage, adult acne, and premature aging due to sun and tanning bed exposure.

Because of my own skin issues, I started looking into options for how to reverse that damage. I started my journey into the med spa world, and was so intrigued by all of the devices and tools that were available for various conditions and anti-aging. I started out using professional skincare, LED light therapy, facials, and chemical peels. Then I worked my way up to various cosmetic laser treatments. I loved ALL of it! I wanted to learn everything I could, and I loved figuring out which products and treatments really worked.

I began looking into schools for esthetics. I loved learning about different ingredients to benefit skin health. I found myself consistently reading books on ingredients, products, and different types of treatments. I made the decision to go to esthetics school in Los Angeles, and from there my journey began. What I found through school was that I loved the focus I had during a facial treatment. I loved how relaxing it was.

The vision that I had for my life was to start a family, be a stay-at-home mom, and have my esthetics career on the side so that I could enjoy a relaxing and calming place, and to earn some extra income. HA! The way it actually went down couldn't have been more opposite!

After I became a licensed esthetician, I discovered my real passion was medical aesthetics. I went on to attend school in Scottsdale, Arizona to become certified as a cosmetic laser technician. I had the most amazing experience at the school I attended. I loved all of my instructors and thought about how great it would be to eventually become an instructor myself. Soon after getting my certification, I moved to Arizona.

Months after I moved to Arizona, I became involved in a relationship that caused me to completely lose myself. I left when my daughter was 8 months old. By the time it was over, I was a complete shell of myself and suffered from severe PTSD. After I left, the real battle began. The next 5 years would entail a 5-year high-conflict family court battle that tested me to my core. During this battle, which consumed me at every level, I was actively pursuing my career in medical aesthetics and doing the heavy work to heal and rebuild myself.

There is something to be said about all the times life knocks you down. What these experiences can teach you is that you have the power to rebuild yourself in whatever ways you choose. You have the power to create whatever life you choose, regardless of the obstacles you're given.

When I left, I had no money, no place to live, and no car. I immediately had to hit the ground running. I began working as an independent contractor at a med spa. I had to build up my own clientele, which was challenging, but it allowed me the freedom to control my own schedule, which was everything as a single mom. I developed a sink-or-swim attitude, and I knew sinking was not an option! I had a daughter to raise, and I wanted to teach her what it looks like to be a strong and independent woman!

As the years went on, I continued my journey of growth. Growth comes with its own set of obstacles, especially in my industry, which is filled with other women who see each other as competition as opposed to seeing the benefit in building one another up. Every obstacle I encountered was merely a learning curve and a steppingstone that would eventually lead me to where I am today.

Over the years, I took on more positions with different clinics, learning more and more from each experience. I was also blessed to have the most amazing clients, some of whom have followed me since the beginning. The last job I took proved to be one of the worst experiences I had ever encountered through a workplace. Then, I lost my job the day Covid hit. Regardless of Covid, I felt as though I could not handle another workplace upset in this industry. I was ready to throw in the towel and give up. Sitting at home alone with my daughter during the shut-down with no income was a scary feeling. After my last experience, I felt major upset and defeat, and decided it was time to make a career change.

I landed on insurance sales. I spent the first few months of the pandemic studying to be an insurance broker. It was brutal for me, because this was not a true area of interest. During this time, I began receiving calls. People were asking if I was still taking clients! This began happening more frequently, and I hated turning them away. After much thinking, I realized that it wasn't time to give up. After all, I truly loved what I did, and knew that I had a gift and a passion for this work!

I worked on changing my thought process and putting out positive energy, which gave me hope for the future of my career. That is when things really started happening for me. Opportunities began rolling in, which made me feel like I was headed in the right direction.

I was offered an opportunity from a previous client to lease a space she owned. She even had spa equipment to help get me started! Another opportunity came my way to be a cosmetic laser instructor at the very school I had attended when I was certified. I began teaching at the same school I had attended 8 years prior. I was able to teach while building my business, which reinforced and improved the skills I had acquired throughout the years. The teaching experience also gave me the confidence to speak in front of others and use my voice to share my knowledge.

A previous client became an investor in my business, which helped me to acquire my first real pieces of equipment! She believed in me, and I knew it was time that I started believing in me too. Having someone believe in me was the biggest motivator for me. After going through so much emotional battering over the years, I had to work extra hard to rediscover my self-esteem and strength. Having someone actually believe in me helped me to grow tremendously. At this point, my business became very real, and I knew that my only path was to move forward, full steam ahead.

I began doing what I did best, which included treatments that got people real results. Medical microneedling, radio frequency skin tightening, medical-grade facials, and medical-grade peels were only a few of those treatments, and I was consistently bringing on new cutting-edge treatments.

I started the process of deciding which products I wanted to bring into my practice. I had worked with all of the top medical skincare lines in my previous years and wanted to make sure that I carried the best products possible. I was approached by a woman who asked if I had ever thought of having my own product line. My wheels started turning; having my own product line seemed unattainable. It felt like another major risk, but I decided once again to take the leap. I discovered a product line that was better than anything I had ever used and I made it my very own! I felt confident offering such amazing products, and I knew that once people tried them, they would fall in love.

My skincare line was a top-notch physician's line with the best medical-grade ingredients. These products delivered results by which I was quickly impressed. My product line began flying off the shelves. My patients loved my products, and they seemed to gain somewhat of a cult following! I began the process of online product sales.

My second year in business, I was ready to bring on my next device. Again, I took another risk...I made the leap! Every step of the way, I have taken risks. With a sink-or-swim attitude, I have been able to do so much more than just staying afloat. My first year in business, I was able to make six figures, with the following year exceeding the previous.

My success has led me to become a full-blown believer in myself and my own capabilities. As a full-time, single mom, my main motivation has been my daughter, who gets to see first-hand all that it takes to be strong and successful. I have always had to be a fighter in order to get through the battles I have been given in life. I have learned that what it truly takes to succeed is to never give up, and to approach each day with humility and gratitude. Growth and pushing through are always at the front of my mind. A little piece of advice: never let anyone make you feel like you're not worthy or capable. Always keep moving in the direction of your passions, and be your own biggest cheerleader. When a passion and a career come together, the sky is the limit.

Favorite Quote

"What you believe, you receive."
- GABRIELLE BERNSTEIN

Recommended Affirmation

I am a magnet for positivity, abundance, and blessings.

Yancey's Special Offer

Thank you for taking the time to learn about me and Face Lounge Aesthetics. I look forward to meeting and working with those of you who are ready to love the skin you're in! Visit me at www.FaceLoungeAZ. com/sixfigurechicks for discounts and more!

About Yancey Taylor

Yancey is a single mom and the founder of Face Lounge Aesthetics, a boutique-style med spa located in Arizona. Aesthetics is her passion, and she strongly believes in only utilizing quality equipment, services, and products with everything she does. Yancey graduated in 2010 from The Academy of Beauty in Los Angeles, where she studied aesthetics. In 2012, she went on to become a licensed Cosmetic Laser Technician. And in 2020, the year she opened her business, she was asked by the National Laser Institute to educate their students on Cosmetic Laser. Now, she has her own medical line of skincare, Face Lounge Skincare.

Overcoming Common Obstacles

In this section, we share our thoughts on how we overcame specific obstacles, challenges, and problems in our lives and our businesses. We've organized the advice and tips by topic, based on the type of challenge we had to overcome. Whether or not you have certain obstacles, we recommend reading through them all to glean advice that may apply to future challenges or other areas of your life.

Overcoming Unworthiness

Katrina Sawa writes: I did doubt my worth in the beginning... even though I could charge more than most, I couldn't get myself to charge what a lot of my friends and peers charged. This was a lesson I'm still learning to this day.

I was confident that I "knew my stuff," as the skills around marketing and sales and client attraction came easy to me. Those skills do not come easily for most entrepreneurs, however, so I did feel confident that others needed my help. I guess I just felt bad for charging too much. Whenever I shared with my parents or friends what I charged for my services, it shocked them a little. No one shamed me, but they were certainly surprised.

These days, I find that value pricing works well for me. When I develop an idea for a program, product, or new service, the price just "comes to me" based on what I believe I should charge, and it usually ends up being a good price. I don't doubt myself, and I never do any research to see what others charge. I just go with my gut. One of the things I tell clients when they ask me what they should charge is, "Charge as much as you can say without stuttering!" *(When you stutter, you lose the sale.)*

Yancey Taylor writes: If you read my chapter, then you already know some of the obstacles I had to overcome. For many years, I was led to believe that I was incapable of doing anything right, that I was worthless. I went through so much; I remember thinking that nobody deserves this kind of treatment. I didn't understand why all of this was happening to me. Why me? I was (and am) a good person, and I deserved so much more. The thing is, it took me a really long time to actually truly believe this. I think there was so much in my life for which I had not forgiven myself, and it was blocking my ability to feel worthy of anything good.

My advice on how to overcome the obstacle of feeling unworthy is to truly know in your heart and truly believe that you deserve more, and that you are worthy of amazing things. Work every day to be a good person and always put your true, authentic self out there. I am a big believer in energy, and I believe that the universe knows if you don't truly believe you are worthy. Once you truly believe it, the universe will start giving you what will feel like miracles. In reality, the universe will reflect back on you those very things which you believe about yourself.

Overcoming Lack of Boundaries

Ashlee McKinnon writes: I am your classic ADHD over-sharer who wears my emotions on my sleeve! I get excited to connect with others, but I can come on too strong or seem like I'm trying to one-up someone else's story or be a know-it-all. The more self-aware I've become, the more self-conscious I've become of this trait. I don't fake it well, nor do I want to.

I didn't understand the necessity of boundaries. I felt that, because I was in the service industry, I needed to be available to all my clients, all the time. I still struggle with this sometimes because I'm so emotionally invested in my clients, and I want to serve them whenever possible. Ultimately, this was counterproductive because it caused me to become physically and mentally drained.

Knowing you need to set boundaries and following through on those boundaries are two different tasks. It was easy for me to say, "The salon phone goes off at 5 p.m. every day," but I still needed to use the phone for email and social media. Then I'd say, "I'm only going to work on my designated days, no exceptions," but my client of 10 years had a family emergency and I could only fit her in on my day off.

For me, I have different levels of boundaries: the non-negotiable ones, and the flexible ones. Thankfully, technology allows me to mute certain settings on my work phone so I can choose which hours of the day I receive specific notifications, and other times I can turn them off. I also started giving myself permission to use certain "free days" to schedule emergency appointments or schedule work-related events. One non-negotiable boundary I've set that has saved me a lot of tears is giving myself permission to cut out toxicity without an explanation.

Carey Conley writes: I have seen so many women struggle with setting boundaries in their businesses and their lives. Learning how to say no to things can be super hard because we have been wired to take on everything we are asked to do. The test for me, when I'm asked to consider a new task or opportunity, is to ask myself, "Does this align with my vision and with the goals I have right now?" If the answer is no, then I decline the opportunity, or else I put it further out on my calendar to consider later. Just because it may be a GOOD thing does not mean it's the BEST thing for me right now.

Julie Jones writes: When I look back on how easily I used to say yes to everything and everyone, I now realize it was a form of self-sabotage. I didn't want to "look bad," and I desired to be viewed by others as a giver. I would say yes to so many people and activities that I had no time for myself and no time to create income within my business. I almost had to forgo surprising my sister-in-law for her 50th birthday party because I had so many "have to's" on my plate. I now easily say no to many things if I know immediately that they are not in my best interest for moving forward. If I am unsure of my decision, I will often ask for 24 hours to consider the "ask" so I have time to contemplate whether it is truly the right opportunity and worthy of a "yes."

Lauren Otto writes: I am a divorce lawyer. I am generally the first person my clients want to call when something goes wrong. Sometimes, things go wrong on evenings and weekends, or in the middle of the night. At the beginning of my career, I was okay with my clients calling me during those moments so I could be there for them in their times of need.

I soon realized that, once you make yourself available for spontaneous calls on evenings and weekends, it is very difficult to reset those boundaries. I stopped giving my clients my cell phone number about a year into my practice. I later stopped taking their spontaneous phone calls and started speaking to people by appointment only. Once clients realize that I am not available at their beck and call, they stop using me as such and generally accept the guidelines of the relationship. Clients who don't accept this policy can move along.

Set your boundaries early in the relationship and BE FIRM. The good clients will respect them and understand the need. The ones who don't are not the clients you want anyway. Your time and your space (and your sanity!) are worth more than the money from clients who disrespect your personal time.

Mel Carr writes: It's not easy to become a six-figure-earning female, but it's definitely possible. I should know, because I am one. When I started my business, I had to overcome many challenges, including setting boundaries. As women, we are often socialized to be "nice" and to put others first. But to be successful, you have to learn to put yourself first and set clear boundaries. Otherwise, you will quickly become overwhelmed and end up burning out. So, how do you set boundaries?

First, you need to clarify your priorities. What are your non-negotiables? Once you know what your priorities are, you need to start saying "no" to things that don't align with those priorities. It's not always easy, but it's necessary if you want to be successful. Trust me, if you can learn to set boundaries and put yourself first, you'll be well on your way to becoming a six-figure earner.

Overcoming Doubt

Alexandria Manning writes: Whether things are going great or things are at a standstill, doubt always finds a way to creep in. During the early months of my business in times of frustration, doubt was a willing and ready friend, telling me it understood and that it was okay to give up. But then this little bubble of hope would always find its way to the surface and whisper to me that I could do it! I loved and hated those hope bubbles! It was so hard; I'd get so tired of trying, but now I'm so grateful for those feelings of hope. Hope gave me the courage to move forward when everything around me was bringing me down with the realities of my circumstances. It wasn't an immediate change, but it helped me move my feet onto a better path that I would otherwise not have found. Still to this day I struggle with doubts. When they come, I acknowledge them as real feelings of fear or worry that I am experiencing and think of how that problem looks and feels solved. I let myself live in that new vision and take action in that new state. If you are trying to solve the problem, while feeling the weight that problem creates you cannot solve it. You need to elevate your thoughts and feelings surrounding that circumstance and instead of telling yourself what could go wrong, start telling yourself what could go miraculously right.

Overcoming Imposter Syndrome

Jen Du Plessis writes: I was a young mother of two, working as a sales rep and calling on other mortgage companies to convince them to use us as a lender. I was at a potential client's office, talking with one of the employees about my family. Suddenly, a gentleman by the name of Vinny launched his chair, rolling himself through his office doorway and grabbing the door frame, leaning into the hallway. Vinny blurted out, "You have kids!" I responded, "Yes, I have two." Vinny said, "If I had known that, I would have given you the business a long time ago. I just thought you were a young chick who blows money partying on weekends." I replied, "No, I am trying to feed my family."

From that moment, I was determined to be myself: a proud young mother, showing off family pictures. I allowed myself to become more vulnerable. My business took off. You can be successful by embracing your truth. So often, during my speaking tours, I see women "pretending" to be men, overcompensating to bring their masculine power to the situation. I'm happy to say that I stopped playing that game years ago, and I still have tremendous power and results in my businesses.

Katrina Sawa writes: Even though I had a lot of confidence in my ability to tell other business owners what to do in the areas of business, marketing, follow-up, and sales processes so they could be successful at their businesses, at times I still felt like an imposter.

I remember feeling like I had a mask on, smiling at networking events while feeling unhappy inside with my starter marriage, my boyfriend in the middle, the amount of money I was making. I felt like I was "faking it until I made it," as the saying goes. I would compare myself to others

72

who did what I did, and I felt like they were always making more money than I was, they had better marketing than I did—and why them? Why not me?

Still to this day I have "Comparison-itis," as I call it. It's very annoying! I wish that I didn't care what others in my industry did, but I do. I'm constantly comparing myself to other women entrepreneurs, even the chicks in this book! I am another work in progress...I'm telling you, we're all still working on something! We're just like you.

Mel Carr writes: I remember one time in a room with six-figure women: I felt smaller than them. I'm a female entrepreneur who has experienced imposter syndrome. I know what it feels like to be a fraud, even though I am successful now. I have worked hard to get where I am, but sometimes I still feel like I'm not good enough.

There are a lot of preconceived notions about what it means to be a successful woman. We are often seen as cold and ruthless, or as people who have to play by different rules than men. This can be tough when trying to build a successful business.

There are times when I feel like an imposter, like people are only supporting me because they feel sorry for me or because they don't think that I can really accomplish much on my own. It's hard not to get discouraged when we are constantly facing these doubts and fears.

But despite all of these challenges, I am still successful. I have built a thriving business and made a difference in the world. And I am proud of that.

Overcoming Fear of Failure

Alexandria Manning writes: In 2019, I was given the opportunity through a friend to go to an exclusive training for business professionals to learn about actual business tools and how to implement them. We literally brought our laptops and did actual work for our businesses while we were there! On the second day, I had a private meeting with one of the coaches. He asked me how the training was going so far, and I told him honestly that it was amazing, except there was one problem: for the business I was currently in, I couldn't use any of the knowledge-built systems, creative strategies, etc. recommended by the trainers.

Then he said something that changed the course of my life forever. He said, "You know what your problem is? Your problem is that you're a CEO, but you're acting like an employee." This rang so true for me that I started balling! It was like I was finally being seen, and I had been given permission to be who I really am. For this training, we each filled out a form about ourselves and our businesses, including our hobbies. The coach looked at my form and said, "Well, it says on here that you love to do interior design." "Oh that?" I replied. "That's just something I do for fun and can do for hours and hours." When he suggested I turn that into a business, I answered in despair, "I couldn't do that as a business; I mean, I live in a tiny town in Utah! How would I even work with clients?"

But his comment got me thinking, and the next day I left the training with Come Alive Interior Design LLC and my first client, whom I had just met while I was there! What holds us back is usually the key to our success if we can just shift our thinking. Albert Einstein said, "We cannot solve our problems with the same thinking we used when we created them." For me, what was holding me back was my location. But that was just my fear of failure talking. Now, I love traveling to serve my clientele and I love returning home to my rural community! For me, it ended up being a win, win. How can you look at what's holding you back in a different way that may give you the answer that enables you to powerfully move forward? You already have everything you need to succeed if you have the courage to stop focusing on your problems in order to more clearly see the solutions.

Jennifer Drago writes: In my mid-50s, as I embarked on my latest entrepreneurial venture, I was shocked when a familiar friend—fear of failure—reared her ugly head. I had fully expected that I wouldn't feel fear at this point in my career, but I was wrong!

I left my corporate role in 2021 and felt that my colleagues and acquaintances would be watching to see where I landed and whether I could be successful in my next venture. I felt pressure to have immediate success as an independent consultant. Fortunately, I was enrolled in a coaching certification program where we did our own inner work so that we could help our coaching clients to do the same. I learned that my fear of failure came from the deeper desire to be admired, successful, and valuable. Since I was starting a business from scratch, it was easy to see why this fear of failure was triggered.

This egoic desire was programmed at a young age, and I learned to accept that this desire was innocent and seeking to keep me safe and secure. From this place, I have learned not to let the fear of failure hold me back from taking action.

Overcoming What Held Me Back

Jennifer Drago writes: As a "recovering" perfectionist, it was very difficult for me to learn to trust others and to delegate work to them. Early in my career as a manager, I held on to projects and worked long hours to complete them, convincing myself that I was helping those I managed by taking on these responsibilities. Plus, I secretly thought I could do the work better and faster than others.

I realized, as I became a more mature leader, that I was actually holding my team members back by not giving them the chance to learn and to show their capabilities and competence. I embraced the idea of delegation and used it as an opportunity to teach, something I love to do. I found that my subordinates were fearful of making mistakes and not meeting my expectations, so I had to have confidence-building discussions, be patient, and be willing to re-educate when issues came up.

I found that it was not only stress-reducing to share the load, but it was fulfilling to teach new things to my team members and to show them that I believed in them. One of the best compliments I have received in my career is that I am a patient and willing teacher, a quality that developed because of my willingness to learn to delegate.

Julie Jones writes: There is a quote from the movie *The Shawshank Redemption* that inspires me in those moments when I doubt whether I even know what the heck I am doing: "Get busy living or get busy dying." Every one of us is either growing or dying. There is no "stagnant" or "stable." As a police officer, I saw how quickly life can change in an instant. There is no promise of tomorrow. We all have an expiration

76

date. I don't want to regret what I didn't do, or those opportunities on which I didn't take the chance, when I take my last breath. I live each day to the fullest. It's a choice for me to have more fun and to take risks. I say "yes" as much as I can to life's opportunities. I don't always have the answers. I just say "yes," and I know that I will figure it out with the support of the people around me.

Overcoming Lack of Confidence

Jen Du Plessis writes: Continuous learning was a crucial part of my success, so I would go to sales seminars to pick up new information. I noticed that some of the gentlemen were constantly getting paged. Yes paged—this was before the iPhone. I thought, "They must be doing very well; they seem to be super-important to their clients." I wondered, "What's wrong with me? I'm just as good—no, better."

Before the next conference, in order to appear successful and in-demand, I asked my husband to page me five times. I was standing in line at the phone bank with the "suits," and when it was my turn, I called my husband. I began talking as if I were speaking with a client. Then, in a much softer voice I would say, "Don't forget to pick up diapers and milk."

Some years later, many of those same men were working for me. Boom! I realized they were not busy at all; they simply did not have control over their businesses. That was when I started developing my proprietary management system. I would never pretend again. Walk in confidence, not in comparison. Those with whom you compare yourself may be themselves pretending.

Remember to be IN demand and not ON demand.

Mel Carr writes: Being a confident woman is key. Having confidence means that you believe in yourself and your abilities, even when others doubt you. It means being able to take risks, speak up for yourself, and handle failure without letting it drag you down. While becoming a six-figure earner will require hard work and dedication, having confidence will give you the extra boost you need to succeed.

Here are four tips that helped me overcome any confidence issues and become the successful woman I knew I was:

- First, surround yourself with positive people who believe in you.

- Second, get rid of any negative self-talk and start building yourself up.

- Third, identify your areas of strength and focus on capitalizing on them.

- And fourth, don't be afraid to take risks; sometimes the best rewards come from taking chances.

By following these tips, you'll be well on your way to overcoming any confidence issues and achieving your goal of becoming a six-figure earner.

Overcoming Self-Sabotage

Jen Du Plessis writes: I can make money, but I can let it go, too. I can overspend, but not on material things, because I am quite frugal. Where I have fallen short is in business. I can be gullible when opportunities for my business present themselves. Why? Because I am so competitive, of course. Because of my past, being a people-pleaser, I sometimes feel the need to say "yes," even if I'm not necessarily interested. Like all of us, I continue to work through these types of challenges. To help myself, I choose one specific word every year to be my beacon of wisdom. From this practice, I've overcome numerous limiting beliefs and self-sabotaging tendencies in my life. Consider increasing your awareness of your actions, decision, and patterns on a regular basis.

Katrina Sawa writes: This is a big one for me, because I had a big ego. I thought I knew best, even when I hired a mentor! They would suggest I develop a new program, price something differently, or even niche way down to doing ONE thing. They all wanted me to niche down what I was coaching. Instead of being a business coach who worked on everything from the big picture all the way down to the nitty gritty of what clients wanted to do, say, send, and post—they wanted me to pick a lane. I was really good with my follow-up, for example, and no one was teaching that at that time. I could have stood out like a sore thumb with that niche, being the "Follow-Up Queen" way back when. But nope, I ignored their advice!

I self-sabotaged my own success and a faster path to more money because I couldn't and wouldn't niche. Looking back, it would have solved all my problems for sure, and I probably could've reached a million-dollar business by 2009 or 2010 if I'd listened to my mentors. (Multiple people gave me this advice, by the way!) I should have trusted them; they knew what I needed, and I should have just done it. My ego got in the way of making more money faster.

Yancey Taylor writes: One of the best parts about my career is getting to talk to different men and women throughout my days. Some of the most common things I hear people talk about are the things they do not like about themselves. Because I am in the beauty and aesthetics industry, I hear mainly what people don't like about their skin and/or bodies. Many times, it doesn't stop there. It's very interesting to hear this kind of talk, and I must say that it has really led me to try and improve the way I talk to myself about myself.

I'm pretty sure that the majority of people on the planet have a little voice in their heads that tells them negative things, like: I'm not good enough, skinny enough, pretty enough, smart enough, nobody likes me...and the list goes on and on. Have you ever noticed that negative self-talk can sometimes be addictive? I know that I am guilty of this self-sabotage type of behavior. It is truly a bad habit. But you know what? Habits can be broken, and you can retrain your mind.

When I notice this negative self-talk creeping up, I find it helpful to stop immediately and replace the negative self-talk with something positive. I prefer to focus on what I am grateful for. If you truly observe your thoughts, you will find that most of the self-sabotaging things that you say to yourself aren't even true! Stop and ask yourself whether what you are observing is even important...does it matter in the big scheme of things? Is this self-sabotage helping you to become the person you aspire to be? If not, then you don't need it! Retrain your mind to think only positive thoughts and bring positivity into your life. What does that look like for you?

Overcoming Gender Biases

Jen Du Plessis writes: All the work was paying off; it was my time to be promoted to Branch Manager. But as it turns out, I was overlooked. I was so angry, I resigned. I was a top producer and contributor; I had the facts to prove it. Within two weeks, they called me and wanted me back. I would be a Branch Manager. But like a version of *Groundhog's Day*, once again I was overlooked, this time for a Regional Manager position. They said it was because my husband worked for the company, so I let my husband go. (One day I will tell the back story to this.)

It didn't matter; I didn't get the promotion. I led with facts and statistics, and spoke to my accomplishments, collaborative nature, and tenure. It was time to soar at a different company, one that appreciated my skills.

My manager at the time, Dave, has been a dear friend and mentor for over 35 years. But I take every opportunity to remind him about the terrible mistake he made by losing me. He agrees with me now, but at the time he said that he "Didn't think the industry, in fact the world, was ready for a woman in that position."

Jennifer Drago writes: I was fortunate to work for several male leaders early in my career who saw my talent and entrusted me with responsibilities that were well beyond what even I thought I could handle. Interestingly, the female leaders for whom I worked (and who were my peers in the later parts of my career) tended to treat me as a competitive threat, instead of as a respected peer or collaborator. In fact, it was primarily my female counterparts who contributed to a highly toxic workplace, acting as bullies and putting up barriers instead of collaborating as fellow executives.

While it may be highly unusual to say this, and I know that other women have had vastly different experiences, all but one of my male superiors encouraged my growth. Similarly, all but one of my male counterparts respected me as an equal. As a result, I personally preferred working with males at the executive level throughout my career.

I firmly believe, as women, we should be better at supporting other women, especially in corporate environments. Because of my experiences, I chose to support the women on my team by promoting their growth and development and by mentoring them. I would not tolerate gossip, drama, or disruptive behaviors. I sought to be the best possible example and role model for the women (and men) whom I led.

Lauren Otto writes: I am a female law firm owner, which is a double whammy when it comes to gender biases. While over half of lawyers are now women, only about 23% of law firm owners are women. I am also a business owner, a category in which women are also the minority. The "old boys club" is very much alive and well among the older male attorney population that is generally in control of the culture and expectations.

I will never forget the day I most strongly felt this prejudice against me, a woman. My oldest was still a baby and happened to be sick that day, so therefore he couldn't go to daycare. My husband was finishing up his master's degree classes and was therefore unavailable to stay home. I had court, so I had to call in because I couldn't leave my son. I remember standing in the kitchen, in court, listening to my baby crying for me in the next room while the judge berated me over the phone for not being there in person. It was the most awful feeling.

I don't think gender bias is something that we just overcome once, and then we are done. It is an ongoing battle. We women must be a little bit smarter, have our s**t a little more together, and run a little bit faster to be perceived as equals by our male counterparts. So just do it. Do whatever you can to affect change for the next generation.

Shari Weller writes: Working in a gender-biased environment is not for the faint of heart. For seven years, I worked in a male-dominated industry. I was paid a fraction of what my male counterparts were paid and boy, there were double standards. At first, I tried not to notice. However, I felt I was always trying to prove myself. I would come in early and stay late, and I always went above and beyond what was required. Eventually, I earned the respect of not only my co-workers, but my distributors and clients. Everything changed, however, when my first son was born. Family became my priority and I started to say "no" to certain things. I was no longer coming into work early or staying late, because I wanted to be home. Even the dads in my company did not understand my choice, because their wives were at home taking care of their kids. The turning point came when I became ill and had to be hospitalized. I realized no job was worth the stress, anxiety, or bias, and once I put myself first, I was able to have the confidence to leave that toxic environment.

Overcoming Social Expectations

Ashlee McKinnon writes: I'm not sure when the social expectation for me to be a stay-at-home mom was placed upon me. But I figure it happened because most of the women with whom I socialized and attended church had grown up with stay-at-home moms and always wanted to be stay-at-home moms themselves. But I never thought I would actually fulfill the expectation that once I had children, or when my husband finished school, I would quit my job.

I love my children and my husband; they are my motivating factors to becoming a better me. But being creative and being surrounded by people bring joy to my soul. And I get to come home and be a more fulfilled version of myself. My home life and my work life challenge me in different ways to learn more, help more, love more, and get to know myself more deeply.

Julie Jones writes: Deep down, there was a time when I was worried about fitting in or being a cool kid. I was bullied in grade school and high school, yet I still had some friends. There were kids in school who did not have friends, and my mission was to never make people feel like they were alone. In college, I started to wear crazy outfits and costumes. I inspired people to have fun and be who they are, not who society expects them to be. I love to wear costumes and crazy googly eyeglasses, and to make people laugh. I show up to networking meetings and Zoom meetings—and I walk around my town—in costume. People often say, "I wish I could do that!" And my answer is, "Why not?" You can still be professional and get things done while having fun and making people smile. People are tired of the "have to's" in life. I want you to remember that there is so much joy in the "get to's" of life.

Overcoming Lack of a Support Network

Carey Conley writes: One of the best things I did to help me keep going early on while starting my first business was to seek out a support network of other women who were a little further ahead in their businesses. I called these people my 'front row' people. They were the ones who believed in my vision, reminded me on the days I really needed it that I was doing great, and gave me the best advice at just the right moments. Too many times, the people we allow to have access to our time and emotions are the people who are not our biggest cheerleaders. To overcome getting discouraged or wanting to quit, you must seek out and create that support network; it's everything!

Lauren Otto writes: When I first started my business, I did everything myself. Not only did I practice law, but I was also the bookkeeper, the billing specialist, the IT specialist, the paralegal, the receptionist, the marketing department, etc. As my client base grew, so did my administrative work, and I soon realized that I was likely losing money by trying to keep up with everything myself. I was faced with the fact that I had to depend on someone else to do the work, and the worries crept in: Would they do the work as well as I did? It really would be quicker if I just did it myself rather than teach someone else to do it, etc.

These worries stopped me from hiring someone, until finally I was drowning in work and the rails were coming off my business. Once I finally hired out the work, I wondered why I had waited so long. When you are trying to decide whether to hire an employee, think about whether you could be spending more of your time on the tasks that make you money so you can make more of it. When you get to the point at which you can make more money than you'll be paying the employee to whom you delegate the work, then it is time to hire someone. Don't let your worries get in the way!

Overcoming Lack of Biz/Life Balance

Alexandria Manning writes: We all have the same amount of time during the day. Only you can determine how to use it. For me, balance looks like being fully present. If I'm with my family, I'm with them. If I'm working, I'm working. Sometimes this mixes together a bit since I work from home, so when my kids interrupt me, I try not to be the parent who says, "I'm busy, go away!" I don't want my kids to feel unimportant, because they are the most important! I'm not perfect though, and I make mistakes. Since I do work from home, I like to spend more quality time with my kids, whether that's going to the aquarium or watching a movie together. I realize they'll all be grown in the blink of an eye, and I don't want to miss it! The hardest part for me was managing the household chores. So now, I have a lady come to clean once or twice a month so that I can focus on my family and my business, and not on the chores. I wonder why I didn't do this sooner!

Carey Conley writes: When I began my entrepreneurial journey, I was a mom with two babies under the age of three and a husband who traveled a lot for work. I had to learn quickly how to balance my home business with my family life. I sought the advice of some other successful work-from-home moms who taught me the importance of time blocking. I learned how to block time in my day to be fully present for my family, and how to stay focused on my business at set times instead of trying to fit it into the 'nooks and crannies.' This eliminated a lot of stress on us all!

Katrina Sawa writes: Because of my previous work ethic, I believed that in order to make more money, I had to work more. I was a work-a-holic for the first dozen years or so. I would often work weekends and, especially when I was single, I never stopped.

In the last few years though, a lot of personal stuff has happened that has caused me to reevaluate how much time we have to live our happiest lives—and how quickly that time can be taken away from us.

My dad died in 2007, which forced me to take a lot of time off to manage his estate, as I was an only child. At that time, I still needed to market regularly to get new clients. It was a real hardship for me to travel and take time off like that. Then in 2012, I had to have two total hip replacements, which took me out of the office again for 3-6 weeks each time. Three weeks after my engagement to my Keeper Husband in 2014, he was diagnosed with throat cancer. We had to travel daily across town for chemo and radiation treatments for 8 full weeks. Thankfully, he's in remission. But that series of events scared me so badly, I knew I had to streamline my business and make sure I spent more quality time with my family and friends.

Lauren Otto writes: We know that the work of the business owner is never done. There is always more marketing we could do, more organizing, more systems to implement, policies to write, etc. We could grow our businesses that much faster and make more money even quicker if we could just be there 24/7.

The reality is, this amount of work is not sustainable. You can only work so hard for a certain amount of time before you completely burn out and can't do it anymore. Growing a business is a marathon, not a sprint, and you need to be able to sustain yourself for the long haul. Having a life outside of your business will help you with this.

My goal has always been to make it home to my family between 5:30 and 6:00 every single night. I am proud to say that I have been able to accomplish this goal at least 80% of the time, and I have a close relationship with my spouse and kids to show for it.

My best advice for accomplishing this goal is to have careful planning and prioritize your tasks. Know the timeline for what you absolutely need to get done, and what can wait. Put everything important on the calendar and stick to your commitments. I did this, and I still built a seven-figure law firm in 11 years. You can do it, too: no excuses.

Overcoming Lack of Ownership for Your Accomplishments

Yancey Taylor writes: There are many times when I sit back and my heart is filled with so much gratitude for where I am today and for the people who have helped me along my journey. I remember having a conversation with my mother during which I told her that I gave all the credit to a dear friend who helped me get to where I am. It is true, my investor significantly helped me to get on my feet, but my mother pointed out a fact. She said to me, "You are where you are today because you have worked your butt off." That hit hard. She was right! My friend and investor helped me significantly by giving me the tools, but I worked hard to make my business come to life and succeed!

Why do I always feel the need to give others the credit for my success? I feel like yes, I have worked my butt off! I have grown and continue to grow a successful and thriving business. I can look back now and see all the work I have done and continue to do, and I am so proud! This business is my passion and it's okay to take credit for its success!

Overcoming a Fear of Asking Questions

Ashlee McKinnon writes: I remember wanting to be a Brand Educator, but I had no idea how to get in contact with the specific brands to apply for those positions. I assumed I first had to have a specific skill level and make a significant amount of money behind the chair, or else have a celebrity clientele. I went years with these assumptions! I finally worked up the courage to ask the educator at a class I attended. Turns out, I just had to ask! Most companies want to train you in their styles, and the less experience you have, the better! I've recognized that, for myself, the scarier the questions seem, the more I need to get the answers. The answers that were "hardest to earn" have been the most rewarding answers in my career and my home life.

Julie Jones writes: This was a big one for me. There have been so many instances in both personal and professional life when I was truly afraid to ask for what I wanted or needed. I think it boiled down to being told "no," which I used to look at as a sign of rejection. Then I heard the saying, "If you don't ask, you don't get," and I put a post-it note on my computer as a reminder that I needed to ask for more of what I wanted. It was also a reminder to me that so many people in my life had asked me for support, and I was always happy to help. In fact, I realized that there were so many people who wanted to support me. They were just waiting and hoping to be asked. Being asked makes people feel valuable and important.

Mel Carr writes: Asking for help is hard. It's even harder when you're a woman trying to make it in a male-dominated field. But if you want to be a successful female, you have to overcome your fears and ask for help. Here are four tips to help you do just that:

- First, don't be afraid to ask questions. If you don't understand something, or if you need clarification on a task, ask.

- Second, when you're feeling overwhelmed or stressed, ask for help. We all have our limits, and there's no shame in admitting that you need assistance.

- Finally, don't be afraid to ask for mentorship or guidance from more experienced people. These people can provide invaluable insights and advice that can help you reach your goals.

- So don't be shy: reach out and ask for help when you need it.

Shari Weller writes: If you've ever heard, "If you want the job done right, do it yourself," that described me to a T. I never asked for help for two reasons. One, I didn't want to impose on others. And two, I always thought I could do it just as well, if not better, myself. As a recovering control freak, asking for help has been a game-changer. No longer do I have to do everything by myself. Furthermore, my new policy has enabled me to empower others to help. I love helping others, and I am always ready to say yes when someone asks me for help. I never realized how much other people like to be asked to help, or how empowering it would be to allow others to help. When it comes to asking for what you want, that's an important fear to overcome. Many people don't ask for what they want for fear they won't get it. After attending a Jack Canfield seminar and reading his book *The Aladdin Factor,* I realized I would never get what I wanted unless I asked. Until you ask, the answer is always "No." The answer may still be "No" once you ask, but asking is the only chance you have at getting a "Yes."

Overcoming Fear of Taking Risks

Shari Weller writes: I would not consider myself a big risk taker; however, I recently left a 17-year business (and income) during a recession to start over. It was probably the biggest risk I have ever taken. The older I get, the more I realize how important it is to stay true to my core values and to live my life to the fullest. While my previous business had provided me with a nice residual income, it had not provided me with joy or fulfillment. I was not looking to start over; however, when the right opportunity presented itself, I knew I had to take the risk. Not only did I risk my financial stability, but I also risked friendships and relationships I had built over almost two decades. I learned quickly who to count on for support, and I learned who my true friends were. While this was a difficult decision, it has also been one of the best decisions I could have made for myself and my family. At the end of the day, it was worth risking the disappointment of others to do what aligned with my vision for the future.

Yancey Taylor writes: Have you heard the saying, "No risk, no reward?" I am a firm believer in this philosophy. When I first started my business, I took many risks. From opening my doors to having an investor and starting my product line, these were all risks. I would never have had any success had I not taken these risks. In my eyes, taking a risk is a win-win, no matter the outcome. If you take a risk and succeed, then you have success. If you take a risk and fail, you have a lesson and an opportunity for growth. Also, if you take a risk and fail, that is just your nudge to try another way. If you go through life waiting for everything to be perfect, you can actually limit your growth opportunity and become complacent.

Overcoming People Who Don't Take You Seriously

Ashlee McKinnon writes: When I introduce myself to new people and I'm with my husband, there is always the assumption that I don't work—especially once they hear we have three children. As if moms haven't been working their tails off since the dawn of time. But when the subject does get brought up and I say, "I do hair," there's a collective, "Aww, that's cute!" response, followed by, "You just play with hair all day, must be hard." "But how do you pay your bills?" "Good thing your husband has a doctorate." It used to really rile me up, and I felt like I had to prove I was more than *just* a hairstylist. I'd rattle off the laundry list of tasks it takes just to get through a consultation or make one Instagram post.

I have been able to separate my own feelings of doubt and imposter syndrome from these types of statements, and I don't take it personally anymore. I've since come to realize that people are meeting us with their own limiting beliefs and limited knowledge outside their realm of experiences. Instead, I love to express how truly blessed we feel as a family to have two incomes, and a partnership that allows us to each explore our individual talents and teach our children to do the same. I try to make light of their comments and engage them in a conversation that will naturally allow me to show and share my business-savvy side.

Shari Weller writes: When people learned I had given up my corporate career to pursue the Network Marketing profession, many people thought I was crazy. Why would I give up a great income, company car, benefits, expense account, etc. for some "little home-based business?" I saw the vision of the network marketing business model immediately. As a marketing major in college, I couldn't believe I had never heard of this type of business. It is an amazing way for ordinary people to do extraordinary things and have an entry into entrepreneurship without the exorbitant startup costs and risks of starting a traditional business. I loved the idea of being my own boss, the unlimited income potential, and the opportunity to coach and train others to do the same. I always treated my business as a serious business, and the naysayers learned that not only was I serious, but my business was serious, too.

Overcoming the Need to be Perfect

Alexandria Manning writes: Wow, this is a big one—and it was the reason I'd often get stuck in my business, especially during the first two years when I was still figuring out my brand and how I wanted things to run. I had a process I created to help my clients' projects run smoothly, but I didn't yet have a system in place that looked something like: sofa from 'x' store, lamps from 'y' store. I was stuck on this for a couple months. Then one day as I was thinking about it while walking down to my garage, I realized: "There is no one-size-fits-all! There is NO system! People are all beautiful, complex puzzles, and I don't want to repeat the same thing over and over. I want to create anew with every client I have!" Oh, the relief I felt! So, from then on, I happily followed a process but with no system, which has given me the freedom to create freshly inspired designs for each client.

We put a lot of unnecessary pressure on ourselves to get things right or to be perfect. When you allow yourself to 'try then tweak' you give space for the answers to come. There's no shame in being yourself, starting where you're at or making mistakes. To quote Miley Cyrus's song *The Climb,* "it's not about how fast you get there, it's not about what's waiting on the other side, it's the climb!"

Jen Du Plessis writes: I did feel the need for perfection, and it held me back. Don't worry about being perfect; just get out there and do it. In fact, I believe imperfection is attractive. Once, I was on stage walking back and forth, and I accidentally stepped right out of my heel. That situation could have thrown me off my game. But it didn't. I acknowledged it, put the shoe back on, and said, "Nothing to see here, just me being me."

You can turn imperfect situations into vulnerable moments. They are real, and your clients, colleagues, audience, and family love them. You become relatable, not fake. I once had a fellow Mastermind colleague tell me that my social media posts were too perfect. She suggested that I post more photos of me without makeup, in casual clothing, etc. My response was that I have plenty of those types of posts, and to be truly authentic, forcing that image for the sake of a few extra "likes" would be very un-authentic for me, and it would feel contrived. My best advice is to do your best, but don't take too much time because if you aren't in front of your client, your competition is winning.

Jennifer Drago writes: For as long as I can remember, I was a perfectionist. I would "overdo" my homework assignments in school and seek straight As to compensate for my lack of confidence. My attachment to perfectionism started to wane during college when I was working full-time and attending school full-time. I realized that I could still get acceptable grades with less effort—I wasn't comfortable accepting less-than-perfect work, but I had to accept that I was doing the best I could do.

When I started my professional career after grad school, I returned to my perfectionist tendencies, wanting to impress my boss, my peers (who were older and more accomplished), and board members. I was late turning in one of my first major projects because of my desire for perfectionism, which led to my first performance improvement discussion. I realized that perfectionism could lead to procrastination.

Today, I am fully accepting of being messy and imperfect, especially in the online entrepreneurial world where we must consistently create content. We can't help but make mistakes from time to time, and it is acceptable to show up vulnerably and to admit our shortcomings. Whenever I feel the tendency to overdo something, I remind myself that "Done is better than perfect."

Overcoming Undervaluing Your Work

Alexandria Manning writes: Knowing how to price correctly for the value I had to offer as an Intuitive Interior Designer and not having the urge to apologize to people for being so 'expensive' was difficult for me, so I underpriced my service for a long time. What I discovered was that, when I priced too low, I would attract clients who were less than ideal. Once I overcame the fear of pricing myself correctly, many things started to fall into place. The clientele with whom I wanted to work started seeking me out, and there was never an issue with my pricing. It's funny how there is always an issue with your pricing when you're not working with the right clientele, and how it magically goes away when they are the right fit. Don't be afraid to price your product or service where the value exchange will be at its most rewarding, for you and for those you serve. It will naturally allow those clients who will drain you to fall away, and those who will uplift and inspire you to serve at your highest level to come pouring in!

Ashlee McKinnon writes: Placing a value on my work has changed through the years. We all work to earn money so we can live and do fun activities. Now, I'm the one in charge, and no one is telling me what to do or what I am "supposed to" charge for my services. How much is too much? What is the competition charging? There are so many opinions.

This was when knowing my numbers really comes in handy. There's is always a basic cost for doing the work. I have to pay the rent and utilities for the building, the cost of the furniture I'm using to perform the services, client comforts, and then the actual product I'm using on each person's head. Add all those numbers together and that's my fixed cost per client. Next, I take how much I want to bring home at the end of the year, divide that number by 12 months, and divide that number by the number of days each month I'm working. Finally, I divide that number by the average number of clients I can see in a day. That's my variable profit per client. I add the fixed costs to the variable per client, and that's how much my service should cost to generate the income I want. I had to let go of "reality" and start reminding myself if I want to be treated like a designer bag, I had to act like one.

Overcoming an Unfavorable Environment

Jennifer Drago writes: I worked in an extremely toxic environment for a decade. I am embarrassed to say that I didn't realize how toxic it was or how damaging it was to my confidence, until after I left. Why did I stay so long? I enjoyed the work I was doing; I held the organization's mission in high regard, and I felt that I was able to make an impact in our community. Most of the time, I was able to compartmentalize and turn a blind eye to the disruptive and antagonistic behaviors my colleagues demonstrated toward me. I felt the need to "prove" that I was stronger, and that others' words couldn't affect me. I eventually chose to leave the organization, but in hindsight I wish I had done so sooner.

Some of the characteristics of this workplace included:

- A lack of support from my executive peers on projects

- Being gaslighted by colleagues

- Being unfairly portrayed in office gossip as cold, demanding, and manipulative despite the associates on my team (who knew me best) saying the opposite

- Receiving no support from my superior when I brought these behaviors to his attention, which allowed them to continue

If you recognize any of these behaviors in your current environment and you are not getting support to change the behaviors, please take my advice and move on as soon as possible. You are worthy beyond measure—don't let others demean you or make you question your value.

Katrina Sawa writes: The biggest obstacle I had to overcome in my personal life was when my "Starter Husband" didn't understand me anymore. Once I learned what else was possible for me, my business, and my life, he just wasn't interested in learning and growing with me, and there was no way I could stay small anymore once I knew and grew more intellectually and emotionally. We grew apart and lost all affection and love for one another; we were basically living like roommates for the last two years in our marriage. I knew that I deserved someone who "got me" and supported me and my new goals 110%. I knew and felt in my heart that I deserved to be loved and supported more than I was, so I left the marriage.

My dad, too, was a second negative influence for me. Although I hardly ever saw him, one minute he would give me a compliment about how great and successful I was and how he was proud of me, and the next minute he'd tear me down with something negative about me. He would do this so often that I just had to spend less time with him, and shortly thereafter he passed away. Removing these two toxic relationships from my life was so freeing! I no longer had to tolerate negative and unsupportive people! And now my "Keeper Husband" totally gets me and supports me through any and all decisions, especially regarding my business.

Overcoming Lack of Family Support

Carey Conley writes: Unfortunately, one of the biggest obstacles we must sometimes overcome is a lack of support from the very people from whom we want it most: our families. This was a big challenge for me, too. Over time, I learned to share with them only if they sincerely asked me how things were going, and even then, I would only share the excitements and progress (even if they were small in the beginning). It isn't that they want to see you fail; it is simply that they don't have your vision of the bigger picture, and they want only the best for you. As much as you can, don't take this personally.

Yancey Taylor writes: Have you heard the saying, "If you want to know who your real friends are, start a business!"? This statement is truth! I didn't really have family support, and I have lost friends along the way in my business journey, which honestly should be expected. I've had friends delete positive reviews they had left for me, expect discounts or free services, not support my social media, judge and make negative comments about my social media, and the list goes on and on.

The bottom line is, none of this has stopped me. You may lose friends along the way, but the truth is, you will make new friends, and most likely they will be friends who are more aligned with your views. They will be the ones who truly support you and your growth in the right ways. Sometimes you assume your friends and family will be your biggest supporters, you should know that your friends and family are not going to be the ones who help you grow your business. Having friends and family support you can feel great. However, you should always be your own biggest cheerleader. If you know that going in, then not having support from friends and family shouldn't come as such a big blow. Always remember that friends will ask for discounts, but true friends will pay full price to support you, your time, and your work.

Overcoming Not Knowing How to Market or Get Clients

Carey Conley writes: Want to know the quickest way to overcome not knowing how to market yourself or get clients? Hire a coach who is a marketing expert for your field! It amazes me how willing we are to try to figure things out on our own, simply because we fear making this investment. I felt the same way until I finally hired my first business coach—and what a difference that made! She taught me her success system, and by following it, I was able to not only get that investment back, but I ended up creating a six-figure revenue within the next year!

Shari Weller writes: I was never taught the importance of networking in school. I have always built quality relationships and friendships and, as an employee of several Fortune 500 companies, I never needed to network. This all changed once I became an entrepreneur! At the beginning, I thought I could build my business strictly through family and friends. Quickly, I realized that in order to grow my business, I would need to grow myself, get out of my comfort zone, and start networking. At first, it was as awkward as going to a high school dance all alone! I was introverted, and I waited for people to come up to me. It didn't take long for me to realize this was not helping me—or my business. I decided to make a game out of it, and my goal for each event was to meet 1 new person. More than 15 years later, I love networking and meeting new people! In fact, many people consider me an expert networker, and now they come to me for advice. I have built a strong business based on networking and referrals, but I was only able to do that once I overcame my fear of networking.

Overcoming a Lack of Courage to Lead

Julie Jones writes: One would think that, after serving as a police officer and on SWAT, I would possess an incredible amount of courage. But in fact, I felt like an imposter in this area. Courage is a feeling that has eluded me for most of my life. I started to take action in areas where I needed to have courage, like skydiving and climbing the Sydney Bridge in Australia. I have a fear of heights, and by facing my fears each time and stepping into action, this powerful feeling would fill my body. I would see what I had just accomplished with these bold actions, and I realized I could take daily steps to build up my courage. I speak up and speak out often from a direct and loving space. In the moments of doubt and fear which I still get from time to time, I ask myself, "What is the worst thing that can happen?" More importantly, I ask myself, "What's the worst thing that could happen for someone else if I don't share my message?" I have a drive to serve humankind, and that's what drives me to step into courage and action.

Mel Carr writes: I'm a six-figure chick and I know what it's like not to have the courage to lead in a situation. When you're starting out, it's easy to be afraid of what people will think or say about you. But you can't let that stop you from going after your dreams. I was always told that I was too shy and needed to be more outgoing if I wanted to be successful. So, I forced myself to "put myself out there" more. I started attending networking events and talking to strangers. It was uncomfortable at first, but eventually, I started to feel more confident. And now, I'm running my own business and making more money than I ever thought possible. So don't be afraid to put yourself out there and seize opportunities when they come your way. Be brave and go after what you want in life. You never know where it might lead you.

Section 3

Best Practices and Advice for Becoming a Six-Figure Chick

In this section, we are giving the best practices and advice we wish we had received early on in our journeys when we were just starting out. These are the things that helped us bring in six figures or more every year!

We've organized the advice and tips by topic, based on the type of HAT we had to wear, activity performed, strategy, and thought process. We recommend reading through them all to glean advice for all areas of business (and life!).

Best Practices & Advice Around Goal Setting

Ashlee McKinnon writes: Once I know how I want to retire, I'm able to work my way backwards from today and build the steps, goals, and benchmarks it will take to get me there. Now, I'm excited for the future! I want to do the work to get there. With my personal goals set, I add in other people. What type of team do I want? What feeling do I want us to have collectively? This is the stage where I select and set boundaries around my work life and home life. What type of work culture do you want to cultivate, and how will you protect that culture? Be picky about who's in the inner circle! At some point in the growth process, doing it alone just won't be an option anymore and you'll need someone who has your vision and who is invested.

Carey Conley writes: There is a secret I've learned, not only on how to set goals, but to ensure you will achieve them. You must write your life vision FIRST! When I was in my late twenties, I discovered that I was not happy working for other people, and I was told by my first mentor that I could have any lifestyle I wanted. I just needed to get crystal-clear on what that lifestyle looked like. So, I took a day off work and, with legal pad and pen in hand, I wrote out in detail what my dream life looked like. This included my family life, how I dreamt of working from home while raising our kids, where we traveled, and most especially, the kind of person and entrepreneurial leader I wanted to be.

Most people have never taken the time to clearly write this out, which means their goals are not 'anchored' in something bigger. This is the main reason why I see so many entrepreneurs struggling with consistency, putting too much on their plates, and most especially, not making money. Once the vision is written, you can break it down into smaller goals with a timeline to achieve them!

Jen Du Plessis writes: Let me ask you a math question. If you set a goal to gain 100 new clients per year, and by June you have 60—what will you do for the rest of the year? Most people will answer that they need 40 more clients to reach the goal. But if you obtained 60 new clients in the first six months, why wouldn't you do the same (or more) in the second six months of the year? In my opinion, "goal" setting may be holding you back.

So, instead of setting goals, focus on client acquisition. How many people do you need to attract to your business each day in order to get to the goal? Focus on your daily activities rather than on the results. You will be amazed at how you not only achieve the goal, but exceed it.

Determine how much revenue you want produce, and why. Be strategic about the average sale. For example, do you want to have numerous clients at a smaller price point, or do you want to work with fewer people at a higher price point? What if you were to procure just 10 clients at $1 million each? Actions and strategy trump goals.

Jennifer Drago writes: As a strategist, I've seen firsthand the value and importance of setting and achieving goals in a business setting. I recommend that leaders embrace goal setting, as it will provide the roadmap to propel their businesses forward. Here are my recommendations:

- First, create a vision narrative, which is a set of 6-10 statements that describe in inspirational terms where you want your business to be three years from now. It can list how many clients you will have, how much revenue and net income you will generate, what your products/services will be, what your team will look like, what you will be known for, and what recognition your brand will have achieved.

- By having that clear vision for three years from now, you will be able to craft annual milestones for years one, two, and three as you move toward that vision. Then, you can crystalize your annual goals for the upcoming year.

- From your annual goals, finalize your goals for the first 90 days. They should include tasks that you will need to complete weekly to achieve your quarterly goals.

- Keep your vision and your goals in front of you and review them each workday.

- Implement weekly accountability to make sure you complete the tasks that will keep you on track toward your quarterly goals. Use a scorecard to track specific actions, and use an accountability partner or business coach to keep you accountable.

- Repeat this process each quarter for maximum success.

Katrina Sawa writes: I've never been a goal-setter, at least not like the people who teach it (i.e., S.M.A.R.T. Goals). I set annual revenue goals and I often put out there how many people I want to register for an event, a program, or how much I want to sell from a certain event—but that's about it.

I'm a list maker. I love lists! So, I put down my To Do's. For me, that's the goal-setting part. I don't write down my goals often; sometimes they'll go on my Vision Board, which I made for many years while I was moving from 5 figures to 6 figures and from 6 figures to multiple 6 figures. I love vision boards. They used to be really fun, back when I had a lot of magazines from which to cut pictures. Now, I have to figure out how to create my vision boards by printing photos. I personally need a physical vision board, but there are virtual ones available.

Another way I plan is by creating Mind Maps. Look it up: it's fun. I use big markers on flip-chart paper, then I stick the completed Mind Map on my office wall. It's a creative way to brainstorm all my projects or pieces/

tasks of a project or program, and it gives me a visual. I also use flip-charts for my Live Big Mastermind when we hold our in-person retreats, and clients love it.

Mel Carr writes: As a six-figure chick entrepreneur, I know the importance of setting goals. Whether it's a short-term goal of landing a new client, or a long-term goal of expanding my business into new markets, having clear and measurable goals is essential to my success. But setting goals is only half the battle. The other half is achieving them.

That's why I make sure to break my goals down into smaller, more manageable steps. I also set deadlines for each step and hold myself accountable by tracking my progress along the way. By following these simple steps, I've been able to achieve even my most ambitious goals. And I'm confident that I can continue to do so as my business continues to scale.

Yancey Taylor writes: Goal setting is an interesting topic for me. I think I probably operate much differently than most. As a single mom and business owner, I am always being pulled in different directions. Sometimes it is challenging for me to stay focused on the task at hand, and I start many projects without completing them. Here is my method for setting goals and getting them accomplished:

- What I like to do is think big. I think of all of the things I dream about accomplishing with my business and where I see it heading. Then, I rewind to the very beginning.

- Choose a notebook to write down your thoughts. Now, write down the steps you think it will take to reach your vision. These include daily goals and tasks, small goals and tasks, and big goals and tasks. Work towards completing as much as you can in a day, even if it's only one thing. No matter what, you should always be making some sort of progress. As you complete tasks, mark them off the list.

- If you're having trouble completing a task or don't know how to accomplish a goal, don't be afraid to talk to others. Talking out your difficulties with another person can spark ideas on how to get you moving toward where you need to be. Also, delegate whenever possible!

- As the years go on, you can look back through your notebooks at all of your completed tasks and how they contributed to your business growth.

Best Practices & Advice Around Having an Attitude of Gratitude

Alexandria Manning writes: Ten years ago, I was so frustrated with my life that it was hard to be grateful for little things. Big things, definitely! I was grateful for my marriage, my kids, and my husband's stable job—but that was about it. I'd hear people tell me to count my blessings in order to change my circumstances, but all that really accomplished was to piss me off. Looking back, I realize they were right! So often, we blame our circumstances for our results, but it's really our thoughts and feelings that affect our results.

Think of it this way. We often hear about people who started out with nothing and were raised in very poor environments, but now they are successful. Yet, others who started out with those circumstances are still in the same circumstances—so what made the difference? My friends, I believe we underestimate our own ability to literally create any kind of life we desire. Gratitude is one of the highest frequencies, and it is a key to unlocking your creative power! I've never liked the phrase "Fake it 'till you make it." I have amended it to say, "Think and feel it before you can create it."

4 Tips to help you cultivate an Attitude of Gratitude, so you can change the results of your circumstances:

- Begin with what you have. Take a moment or two and write down blessings you have already been given. You can even make this a nightly ritual by keeping a Gratitude Journal. It doesn't have to be perfect. Just write 3 things a day for which you are grateful.

- Spend time in service. This may be volunteering at a soup kitchen or helping an elderly neighbor with their yard care or grocery shopping. Big or small, do something that has absolutely no monetary reward in it for you.

- Gain perspective. Try something as easy as experiencing nature, or more exotic like visiting a foreign country. There's nothing like broadening your perspective to help you cultivate an attitude of gratitude for what you've been given.

- Start being grateful for what you haven't yet been given. I know it may sound odd, but being grateful now for things you will have later will help attract them into your life even faster!

Carey Conley writes: I think if there was one thing that was an absolute game changer in my life, it was having an Attitude of Gratitude. It is so easy to be grateful when things all seem to be going our way, but it is much harder when we are facing challenges. I have learned this through many challenges and losses in my own life. I have built two businesses, and with that, there have been a lot of ups and downs, plenty of mistakes made, financial losses, people disappointing me, and flat-out rejection. Three years apart, my husband and son took their own lives. Every setback and tragedy has been a test of my faith. My faith and my practice of gratitude have gotten me through the trials. It has become non-negotiable in my life to start my day in quiet time with prayer, meditation, reading, and writing down everything I am grateful for that day. No matter how I feel when I wake up, this practice puts me in the right mindset to face the day with joy and a positive attitude.

Shari Weller writes: It's been said that you can't feel emotions such as anger, fear, sadness, comparison, etc. when you are focusing on gratitude. Even during the darkest days, gratitude can shine a light. If I find myself going down a "woe is me" path, I like to make a conscious effort to focus on gratitude. The best time for me to focus on gratitude is the morning, but I also like to remember gratitude before I go to bed.

- Go on a gratitude walk. Be mindful of the beauty surrounding you, and take notice of everything around you. There will be something to make you feel grateful!

- Keep a gratitude journal, and each day, choose a few things to be grateful for. Or use it when gratitude comes to mind.

- Have an accountability partner and set up a time daily/weekly to share gratitude.

- When you are going down the wrong path in your mind, flip your situation into gratitude. I.e., If you are stuck in traffic and stressed about being late, you can be grateful you have a car, and it will eventually get you safely to your destination.

Best Practices & Advice Around Personal Finance

Jen Du Plessis writes: Pay yourself first. This principle may be difficult to achieve as a new business, because you may find yourself scraping for every dollar to reinvest. I get that. I was there, and as with any new business venture, sometimes I struggled too. Make it a point to allocate 10-30% of every dollar you make to savings and/or investing.

We have all heard about working 'in' and 'on' our businesses, but I wanted to work "above and beyond" mine. In the book *Rich Dad Poor Dad*, by Robert Kiyosaki and Sharon Lechter, the four Cash Flow quadrants are introduced to the world. The concept in the book is as follows:

- Employees have a job and trade hours for dollars.

- Self-employed individuals created their own job, so again they are trading hours for dollars.

- Business owners own a system, have a team, and therefore have more freedom with their time by monetizing the system.

- Investors own their investments and all decisions related to them, so money can work for them while they sleep.

You deserve to build a nest egg and a powerful team to support you as you begin moving into the realm of working not only above, but beyond, your business.

Best Practices & Advice Around Wealth Building

Jennifer Drago writes: Here are my five main tips:

- Pay off credit cards and don't use them as debt instruments. My husband and I have maintained a practice of using credit cards primarily to rack up points/rewards or occasionally to take advantage of a same-as-cash arrangement on a high-ticket item. We routinely pay off our credit cards as soon as they are due.

- Make additional principal payments on your mortgage as you are able. We did so, and were able to maximize our equity in our properties as a result.

- Maximize your retirement savings. We have always maxed out what we could contribute to our retirement accounts. I don't believe that saving for retirement gets enough discussion these days, but it needs to be a focus, especially during your wealth-building years.

- Find an investment advisor you can trust. A good advisor will always keep you focused on your wealth goals and show you where you are in relation to those goals at least quarterly. They will help you adjust your investments, if necessary, based on market conditions. Recently, we needed to change advisors and we undertook an interview process to make the decision. Going through this process was eye-opening!

- Most importantly, we did not spend over our limits. We realized early in our marriage that we did not want to be toy collectors or own expensive cars, a boat, and four-wheel utility vehicles. We didn't need to have the latest designer clothes or watches. We wanted to build our wealth responsibly and have a comfortable retirement. This has been our focus for over 30 years.

Julie Jones Writes: One of the phrases my father used to say when I was growing up was "The rich get richer and the poor get poorer" It was the tone in which he would say it that led me to believe for a long time that if you had money, it somehow made you evil. Wealth building starts with your mindset of there is plenty of abundance for all of us. Some of the key factors that have helped me along the way include:

1. Building that positive mindset through reading, audios, podcasts, etc. Some of my favorite books include You are a Badass at Making Money by Jen Sincero, Secrets of the Millionaire Mind by T Harv Eckert and Think and Grow Rich by Napoleon Hill.

2. I have created multiple streams of income and have money work for me. I have rental property, residual income, a wide range of investments, and a pension that I started to collect when I was eligible. I can take my pension money and invest to create even more cash flow.

3. I am always on a journey of learning, and I ask questions when I am uncertain. I don't worry about how I look.

4. I don't prejudge opportunities. If I am approached or offered a wealth building opportunity, I take the time to at least listen and gather information before I say no.

Yancey Taylor writes: Do you believe in manifesting? I have to say, I'm a believer. When I first started my business, it was obviously a building process. I always wanted to do financially better than I had the month before, because it showed growth. When I started seeing my numbers grow, I was beyond thrilled. I received a piece of advice that I will never forget, because it worked! I will share that with you here.

You can start with the amount you make in a month. Let's say you made $15,000 this month. Pick a number that you would like to exceed. For example, if you made $15,000 (or whatever number it may be), tell yourself that you would like to make $20,000. Every day when you wake up, take a piece of paper and a pen or pencil and write these words:

I ENJOY MAKING $20,000 OR MORE EVERY MONTH!

Write this down 20 times on a piece of paper, and say it out loud or to yourself 20 times. As your numbers start to go up, then increase your goal number. Once you've reached your goal, change what you write. After you hit your goal of $20,000, change it to $25,000:

I ENJOY MAKING $25,000 OR MORE EVERY MONTH!

Follow this with $30,000, and so on. If this doesn't happen for you immediately, just keep it up until it happens, and watch your numbers grow!

Best Practices & Advice Around Marketing

Ashlee McKinnon writes: When I started working, I thought my biggest accomplishment would be applying a full head of foils in less than 2 hours. I would work hard, and my skills would speak for themselves, and my chair would never be empty. Reality just wasn't the same! I learned I was in charge of finding the clients I wanted to work with, and sometimes not taking a client was worth more than just taking anyone to make money.

I used a vision board to "meet" the ideal client with whom I wanted to work. I named her Mikayla. I put on my board the type of lifestyle she had. I included the different activities and hobbies she liked, the stores where she shopped, and her favorite colors. I built my marketing strategy around that vision client. The posts I made on socials, on my website, and through my email blasts were all to Mikayla. When I felt like I was talking directly to my "real-life" ideal client, the words came easier.

Set your goals, make a plan, market the crap out of yourself, build your tribe, and enjoy the ride!

Katrina Sawa writes: Marketing is my jam. Over the past 20 years, I've invested more time and energy learning how to do better at marketing than any other element of my business. Also, because I teach my entrepreneur clients how to market, I just love finding new ways to reach more people, to attract them to my free gifts and trainings, and to entice them to register for my events and get on calls with me. Marketing is the fuel of your business; without effective marketing, your sales will dwindle and you won't have a business.

Marketing has changed a lot since I started. When I began in 2002, all we focused on was networking and following up by phone and email. There was no such thing as social media back then. And to this day, I still follow up using direct mail (yes, with a stamp!). I have discovered, especially since everyone is so focused on getting clients from social media and video, that direct mail can be more effective for getting your message into the hands of your ideal prospects—something you want them to see or act upon. Emails go into spam or trash, and you can't guarantee that any of your followers will ever see your online posts.

My main marketing strategy, however, is speaking. Speaking is the fastest path to cash! When you can entertain, educate, and connect with an audience of your ideal clients, you can move them to action so much faster. Don't be afraid of speaking; just clarify what you're speaking about, why, to whom, and what outcome you want to achieve. If you have a reasonably priced program or offering, you can make tens of thousands of dollars with speaking.

Networking today, online and virtually on Zoom, is also still one of my second-favorite marketing strategies. I use the same strategies and consultative approach online as I used in person years ago. In addition, I love traveling and/or hosting conferences and events at least 3 to 5 times a year. They fill me up emotionally, as I can make such a deeper a connection when I'm in person.

Lauren Otto writes: One of the biggest hurdles I had to overcome when I first started my business was the money aspect of a successful marketing campaign. It was not hard for me to learn the goal of marketing, that the money invested would be returned to me in the form of sales to customers. But the *mindset* around investing that money first and seeing the return on it later has been much more difficult to master.

The truth is, I don't think I will ever fully master it, because there is always uncertainty regarding the success of marketing dollars. In other words, there is *always* risk involved, no matter how well-targeted and executed your marketing campaign is. Yet, it is a risk you need to take in order to grow your business, so this is where the mindset piece comes in.

You must have the right mindset about the money you are investing in your marketing so you will make decisions based upon evidence and facts instead of emotions and fear. Seek whatever business coaching and/or mentorship you need to help with your mindset around this. I've never regretted a single dollar I have spent on good business coaching. You won't either.

Yancey Taylor writes: When it comes to marketing, there is no one-size-fits all. I have tried many different types of marketing for my business, from Google ads to ramping up my social media. What works best for you might not be what is best for others. I have found that it is important to give them all a try and see which one returns the most value. This is still a learning game for me, but I know that any type of marketing can help get your name out there. Here are a few ideas to get you going:

- Word-of-Mouth & Referrals - This is, hands-down, the number one form of marketing and advertising, and the highest form of a compliment to your business. I have been blessed to get a lot of this in my business. The best way to achieve this is to always give the best possible service, and to build client relationships.

- Google Ads - Google ads can be very good. Google allows you to set search terms that are relevant to your business so people who are specifically looking for a service you offer can find you.

- Social Media - Putting yourself out there can be very scary, but as the face of a brand it is a necessary evil! It is best to hire a social media manager. Social media can help to build brand awareness and recognition.

- Community Networking - Getting out in the community can greatly help your business thrive. Whether it's through networking groups or organizing a company get-together, networking within your own community can get the word out about what you do.

- Sponsorships - Connect your business with organizations that you feel strongly about so that you can give back to your community. Donate a certain amount of your proceeds to go back to an organization that you care about.

- Local Publications - I have yet to do this one. I think it's great to be in magazines, but I believe that this method of marketing is best for building credibility. This method can also be very costly.

- Brand Advertising - Brand advertising is a great way to build brand awareness. This won't necessarily bring traffic through your door, but it will help people begin to recognize your business through seeing banner ads with your logo and whatever else you choose to show.

Best Practices & Advice Around Hiring & Managing a Team

Ashlee McKinnon writes: With my personal goals set, I add in other people. What type of team do I want? What feeling do I want us to have collectively? This is the stage where I select and set boundaries around my work life and home life. What type of work culture do you want to cultivate, and how will you protect that culture? Be picky about who's in the inner circle! At some point in the growth process, doing it alone just won't be an option anymore and you'll need someone who has your vision and who is invested.

Katrina Sawa writes: Boy, this is a very important topic! It's almost as important as marketing for obtaining clients, and certainly for running a successful 6-figure business. Heck, you may not even GET to 6 figures if you don't hire a team before business starts to really pick up!

Yes, I understand that most entrepreneurs think they must make more money before they "can afford" to hire an assistant or a team. But that is completely wrong! Trust me, early on in your business, the sooner you realize there are things you don't like to do, don't want to do, or don't know how to do, that is when you need to start delegating.

- If you're not a website designer or graphically capable, please DO NOT design and build your own website.

- If you're not a bookkeeper or you don't understand how to do QuickBooks, maximize your taxes and deductibles without reading a 400-page tax manual; please DO NOT do your own books, accounting, or taxes. Do not take a class to learn it or buy the software to attempt to fit it in; just outsource it. You will make more money (or save it!) easily.

- If you don't know how to design effective and "good looking," sales-oriented marketing materials, social memes, and PowerPoint presentations, DO NOT do these yourself; hire a graphic artist, a designer, or a marketing consultant/coach to guide you.

Lauren Otto writes: Believe it or not, attorney-business owners are notoriously cheap. I've talked to many over the years (usually in the context of complaining that they are difficult to get ahold of) about the need to hire a paralegal so they can have a better handle on their caseloads. The most common response I get is, "I don't want to pay someone else money to do something I can do myself."

I just shake my head at them, because they do not realize that refusing to hire a paralegal is *costing* them money. Why is that? Because they are stuck doing tasks that do not make them money, yet are necessary for the successful functioning of the business, i.e., invoicing, bookkeeping, filing, answering the phone, etc. The more time an attorney spends doing work for which they can bill clients, the more money they make.

If this isn't already true in your business, it will become true. Keep careful track of your time for a week to see where you are spending it. Are you are sacrificing the work that makes you money in order to take care of the things that don't? If your answer to this question is "yes," it is time to hire and delegate. Be decisive, and just do it.

Best Practices & Advice Around Asking for Support

Ashlee McKinnon Writes: Give yourself permission to ask for help, whether it's from your partner in life, family, friends, someone who is already doing what you want to be doing, or the internet. Asking for help also allows others to serve you and give back to you. It strengthens bonds and builds a community around you. Networking events are great for this. You're typically surrounded by likeminded people who are at different points along their journeys.

Lauren Otto writes: We entrepreneurial types are a different breed; we think differently than people who are employees. As a result, I have always found it difficult to find people who truly understand me and how I tick. Don't get me wrong, I have plenty of friends who are employees and I do not think any less of them; we simply come from different places and have different concerns.

I don't care what anyone else tells you: being an entrepreneur is HARD. There are many, many benefits to it and I wouldn't trade it for the world, but it is still hard. We jump off the proverbial cliff and figure out how to fly on the way down, and it takes a lot of mental work to keep our heads as we do it. You NEED support to get you through. Find your inner circle and reach out to them when you need them.

I also can't adequately emphasize the benefits of hiring a business coach. These are people who "get it," who can help you do the mindset work you need to. They help get you in the right mindset to make decisions from the right space, and they help get you back there when you go astray.

Best Practices & Advice Around Scaling Strategies

Alexandria Manning writes: For years, I thought that if I wanted something to happen, I had to just go make it happen! I was trying to force it to happen, and I was also trying to force myself to become someone I didn't like in order to get it. Those were hard years for me and my family. I was working hard, doing everything my upline told me to do, and it still did not bring me the results I was after. As I've stepped into what I feel I've been called to do, I see that my ideas about timing have changed. Understanding timing and how to make it work for me is not something I've completely mastered, but through my experiences I have learned a lot, which I'd like to share with you.

What I've learned about timing:

- There is such a thing as perfect timing. For me, opportunities opened up when I became clear about what I wanted to create and stopped listening to other people's opinions on how I ought to create it.

- Thank God not everything works out—and I mean that literally! I'd get so frustrated at God for not bringing me "blessings" for which I was working my butt off! Now, I'm so grateful knowing that He has bigger and better plans for me than I have for myself, and He has allowed for certain things to fail so others can go right—in His perfect timing.

- If at first, second, third, and fourth, you don't succeed...take the hint and move on! This was a tough one, because I hate quitting things! Once I humbled myself and got real about what made me happy and who I wanted to become, I was able to move forward with courage. I let go of some opportunities I cared about and some people I wanted to care about. It was like letting go of an anchor I hadn't consciously realized was there.

Jen Du Plessis writes: Most small business owners are great at the technical aspect of their skill, but very few, if any, receive the proper training in recruiting, hiring, and management as part of their leadership skills. The best social media marketer does not make the best social media marketing company owner.

How often have you found yourself finger-pointing at an employee who isn't working out for you, rather than thumb-pointing to yourself for the lack of leadership, support, and direction to help that employee to be successful? The result is massive turnover, working longer hours, re-working tasks and assignments, and then starting the hiring process once again. All of this frustration and extra work can be reduced with the right leadership skills on your part.

There are seven skills I teach to help people scale their businesses. It's called Smart Scaling, and it consists of the following modalities to level up business owner skills:

- Define your dream team and their specific roles

- Key Performance Indicators (KPIs), Lead, and Lag Indicators signal when to hire

- Talent Scouting techniques and systems

- Interview and hiring procedures and techniques

- DISC Assessments for team culture and breadth

- Utilization of the Management/Leadership Cycle

- Situational Leadership skill development

Best Practices & Advice Around Managing Self-Care

Jennifer Drago writes: Entrepreneurs and business leaders need to be very mindful of their self-care patterns and tendencies. In my experience, women in particular tend to neglect their own needs and health in order to take care of their spouses, families, and businesses. The challenge for women is that if we don't have adequate sleep, nutrition, or physical activity and we don't take time to relax and de-stress, we can't care for our loved ones or our businesses in the way we want.

Here are my tips for prioritizing self-care:

- Implement a morning routine that allows you to enter your day in a calm manner. Some activities might include meditation, journaling, prayer, and/or reading.

- Ensure you are prioritizing sleep and using good sleep hygiene patterns.

- Eat wholesome food and minimize sugar and processed foods. As we all know, garbage in, garbage out.

- Prioritize some form of physical activity every day, in nature if possible.

- Have a workday shutdown routine that allows you to mentally "close the door" on your work, while preparing a short list of priorities for the next morning. Avoid working at night and on the weekends so that you can be present with your family and friends while recharging your energy and creativity.

Shari Weller writes: As a busy mom and a recovering people-pleaser, it took me a long time to be able to leverage my self-care and make it a priority. At first, I took small steps, like getting the occasional massage or scheduling a girls' day or girls' night out. As I started growing my business, I made my self-care more of a priority.

Now, my self-care, personal fitness, and nutrition have become a top priority! They have made me a better wife and mom and a better friend, as well as a happy and healthy business owner.

- Make yourself a priority! Schedule time in your calendar each day. At first it may just be a 5-minute meditation.

- Meal prep healthy meals/snacks, and take supplements.

- Schedule time to exercise; even a 30-minute walk each day will make you feel better.

- Surround yourself with positive people. Negative people will deplete you of energy.

- Read or listen to something positive every day.

Best Practices & Advice Around Networking

Alexandria Manning writes: Honestly, I'm still working on improving my networking skills. I was initially taught many incorrect methods for how to attract and lead people, and it took me a long time to unlearn them. I do know that if you don't have a goal when networking, you're just meeting a lot of people with their own way of doing things, and it's easy to get tossed to and from this opinion or that one. Networking is an art, and people are the canvas. When I network at events, I like to get to know people, engage them in conversation, and listen to my intuition to see if I'd want to set up a meeting or move on. As I navigate through how to use networking to grow my business, I've learned some things to do and some things not to do. Here are a couple of guides that continue to serve me.

My dos and don'ts for networking:

- **Don't** - Work out of desperation. There is a certain kind of stench when someone is working in desperation. I know, because I have worked out of desperation while networking and then wondered why no one wanted to talk to me. When you are desperate, you will find that a lot of your efforts in networking won't go very far, if they go anywhere at all, and you can damage relationships before they've even had a chance to form.

- **Do** - Want to genuinely get to know people. Have you ever had someone come up to you and ask you their 'get-to-know-you' questions, only to immediately ask you to do something for them? You can tell when someone is being genuine or not, so be one of the genuine ones. One solid relationship you form through networking and continue to cultivate over time can

133

bring you a lifelong friend as well as immeasurable avenues of success and support.

Carey Conley writes: Before there was all the online marketing and social media to market your business, I built two businesses to six figures, mostly out of the relationships I had already formed, and through networking. I still believe in this activity, if it is done with the right intention and with a process for how to utilize your relationship-building and your time. Too often when people network, they see it as a time to simply show up, tell everyone all about what they do, take some cards, and leave it at that. That can lead to feeling like you are working on lot, but it's 'not working.' When I choose to network (and I am very selective about where I network), I have an intention to:

- Be more interested than interesting. I am there to build relationships. I want to learn how I can help others vs. how I get them to buy something or be my next client.

- Look for opportunities to collaborate. How can we work together on something?

- What do I have coming up to which I could lead them, if it looks like what I do adds value to their life/business?

Lastly, detach from the result and have fun!

Jen Du Plessis writes: Please don't go to networking events to find business. Go there to find potential collaboration partners who may become clients or who can potentially refer clients to you.

Here is a quick checklist of things to consider when attending a networking event:

- Who will be attending? Contact the event planner to see if there is someone they can introduce you to as a potential partner.

- Attend with a specific intention to meet one or two people with whom you can develop a strong opportunity...then leave. Do not become a networking junkie!

- Schedule meetings while you are there. We all have our cell phones with us. Then, all you have left to do is to confirm the meetings.

- Do not be the first one there, or the last one to leave.

- Do not have more than two cocktails. This is a big business and credibility flaw.

- Leave white space the next day for any follow-through.

- Suggested conversation outline:

    1. Tell me about yourself.

    2. How would I know if I ran across somebody that would be helpful to your business? Respond with:

        1. I may be the person.

        2. I may know a person.

        3. I can research a person.

Julie Jones writes: People will do business with people they have built a relationship with. Networking is an investment of time and in people. Here are some key points that will help you to be an effective networker:

1. It's not what you say. It's how you say it. Be energetic in your delivery. Smile. Have fun!

2. Be interested, not interesting. The conversation should be mostly about them. This is not an opportunity to sell. It's an opportunity to connect.

3. Be unique and memorable. When I am asked what I do for a living, my response is, "I look good, what do you do?" It always gets a laugh, and the conversation is now about them.

4. Offer to help and support with connections and referrals. Helping others first goes a long way.

5. Follow up! We have all heard that the fortune is in the follow-up. If you don't plan to follow up, you are wasting your time. Why even network? Also, the follow-up doesn't always have to be about business. Make it personal as well to show how much you care.

Katrina Sawa writes: Networking is one of my top marketing strategies, and has been for all 20 years I've been in business. Why? Because you can connect with, like, and trust people much faster than you can over social media, for example. I like faster ways to reach more people and get them to trust me enough to want to have a conversation with me about helping them jumpstart their businesses. A couple tips about how to network more affordably and effectively are:

- Go with a goal – Know who you want to meet and why. Look for ideal prospects, speaking opportunities, and joint venture partners.

- Be prepared – Have your marketing materials, books, business cards, and a way to take orders if you're in person. Have free downloads, landing pages, easy links, and enticing blurbs to post when in Zoom meetings and calls.

- Have a follow-up plan – If you're in person, have a plan to enter all the contacts you meet into your database or a way to electronically get them on your list right on the spot. If you're on virtual calls and events, prewrite your autoresponder emails. Add videos to all your pages so people can get to know you further, along with links and buttons to take the next step.

- Work the room – Be intuitive and curious at events, reach out or walk up to say hello to those you want to meet. Don't be shy; you won't get anywhere if you aren't a little more assertive.

Lauren Otto writes: My work as a family law attorney primarily involves "B to C" (business to consumer) marketing, as opposed to "B to B" (business to business) marketing. Very few of my clients are repeat clients, unless they happen to have more issues down the road and they need an attorney for personal reasons, not business-related. I tried networking to get clients early in my business. I joined networking groups, attended events, and got my name out there as much as possible, but I don't think I got a single client lead from it. Given the nature of the work I do, it is also understandable that people do not want to talk about anything related to that at a networking event. I stopped networking for clients after a couple of years, and my business continued to grow and thrive without it.

The amount of time you spend networking should be directly related to its purpose for your business. Further, you need to be strategic with the groups in which you network; tailor your efforts to your purpose. Networking could be a great way to spend your time, depending on your business and purpose, or it could be a big waste of time if it's not relevant to what you do.

Best Practices & Advice Around Public Speaking

Julie Jones writes: I am grateful that I feed off the energy of being in front of a room filled with people. Most people have an immense fear of public speaking, yet I thrive off the ability to deliver an impactful message in front of a room. Some key points of which I remind my clients when I am supporting them in their presentations are:

- Engage your audience with a personal story. The audience wants to know who you are and why they should trust you.

- You are the expert in what you are saying. The audience doesn't know what they don't know. Heck, they don't even know what you are going to say. What you do have to say is perfect for that moment.

- Pause after making a powerful statement. Let the information sit with your audience. Let them feel the emotional aspect of what you are sharing.

- Be genuine. Be honest. Be vulnerable and add humor to your content. It creates even more of a connection with your audience.

- Have fun!

Katrina Sawa writes: My favorite way to share my message, connect with prospects, and generate leads and clients is via speaking. I used to travel all over the U.S. and Canada to speak to groups of 20-3,000 people. During the pandemic, it proved to be even more successful to save money on all that travel, stay home, and speak on virtual events. It's a blessing and a curse because I love connecting with people in person.

I do think that holding my own events in person is a lot more profitable than holding virtual events, but others disagree. With speaking, you want to:

- Be prepared with your talk titles, descriptions, bullet points, bios, and headshot.

- Seek speaking opportunities that are a good fit for you; it is worth spending time searching the internet to find them and apply. I apply for big conferences too, even if I don't feel as qualified as previous years' speakers. You never know until you try.

- Ask event and podcast hosts if you can be a guest. Don't sit idly by and hope they will invite you. Share how you can show value with their audiences. Make it about them, not you.

- Make sure not to be pushy with the speaker bookers; it's their stage. They won't care about you until you care about them and their purpose. (I know this because I book speakers for my International Speaker Network monthly calls and conferences.)

- Connect with the audience, first and foremost...your amazing content comes second. Build engagement, exercises, and even entertainment into your talks.

- Stay on time! Don't go overtime or ask for more time in the middle of your talk; no speaker booker will have you back or refer you if you do this.

Best Practices & Advice Around Attaining Work / Life Balance

Carey Conley writes: Balancing career and family have always been such a challenge for most women. They can feel guilty if they are working too much, and guilty if they feel like they are not working enough. We are our worst inner critics in this area! This leads us to putting ourselves last when it comes to self-care and keeping our own cups filled. Finding your work/life balance takes some focus, but it can be done! First, you must get good at saying 'no' to anything and everything that is not the BEST thing for you to be doing.

Take regular assessments by ranking yourself on a scale of one to five to see how you are doing in these areas: (5 = great, 1= needs a lot of work)

- Faith/Community

- Family

- Friends

- Fitness/Health

- Finances

- Field/Career

- Fun

Make an intentional commitment to really work a little bit every day on the areas that need attention. Where we get off-balance is that we gravitate easily towards putting a lot of time into the areas that come more naturally to us, and we avoid the areas that need the most attention.

Balance is about awareness and caring enough about ourselves to be as whole and well-rounded as possible.

Julie Jones writes: Remember this…magic happens at the extremes in life. There is no idea of work/life balance. You will automatically go out of balance when you are taking action on a priority. Replace the idea of balance with counterbalance.

Here are the things I implement and remind clients when they are struggling with this concept. Trust me, I struggle too!

- Know what the Big Picture Focus is for you. What is the one big thing that you are driven to accomplish? What lights you up?

- What is your small focus? What is your "right now?" Whenever you are about to take action, ask yourself, "Is this moving me towards my big picture or away from it?"

- Be "in the moment" with what is in front of you. If you are working, focus in and don't get distracted. We are not designed to multi-task, no matter how well you think you are doing. When you are with friends and family, be present! It's so easy to tell yourself, "I am going to just respond quickly to this text/email," and then find you've just spent an hour on work instead of with your family.

- Incorporate more fun! If you are not having fun with work or with life, there is a HUGE part that you are missing out on. Learn to laugh more and enjoy the journey. Just doing "one more thing" will create missed opportunities and experiences in life.

Best Practices & Advice Around Utilizing Technology

Mel Carr writes: Utilizing technology has been the key to my success as a successful female entrepreneur. I'm able to connect with my clients and customers 24/7, which has helped me to build strong relationships and grow my business. Additionally, technology has allowed me to automate many of my business processes, which has saved me time and money. I believe that if you're not utilizing technology in your business, you're missing out on a powerful tool that can help you to achieve your goals. If you're not sure where to start, there are plenty of resources available online and offline to help you get started. Utilizing technology is the key to success in today's business world.

Lauren Otto writes: I have always embraced technology in my business because I find that it makes life easier, and my business runs more efficiently. If you are not a technology expert, contract with someone who is to make sure your technological systems are set up correctly to suit your needs. You also want to keep growth in mind when setting up your systems. While it would be overkill to set up your system to accommodate 50 employees when you only have one (or none), you will want to discuss your scaling goals with your technology expert to make sure your technology will be able to scale with you.

Technology has come a long way, even since I started my business in 2011. There are a lot of programs out there that can integrate and interact with other programs to automate tasks that used to have to be performed manually. The more processes you can automate, the less time you have to spend doing them and the fewer staff you have to hire to do them for you. This is also why you should have at least a functional knowledge of the technology that is available, so you can use that knowledge to make decisions about your systems. Technology can be your best friend. Treat it that way!

Shari Weller writes: If used properly, technology can make a tremendous difference in business. It can be a significant time-saver. Technology is essential for my business. I use technology in many different areas, from social media to organizing my calendar to scheduling appointments and literally running my business from my smart phone.

It's imperative to stay on top of the latest and greatest technological advancements.

- Have a presence on the social media platforms that make the most sense for you and your target audience. I've picked 3 platforms that best suit me and my demographics. I am working to be consistent, so people can get to know both me and my business. If social media is not your jam, hire someone to help you!

- Use a scheduling tool for appointments. I use Calendly.

- For organization, I use a ReMarkable tablet to take and organize my notes. This has been a huge asset, as I no longer have to search for notebooks!

- I prefer in-person meetings; however, to maximize time, utilize Zoom or other video conferencing. These options are great if your business can be run virtually and globally.

Best Practices & Advice Around Collaboration

Carey Conley writes: Collaboration is one of my top core values! I love seeing ways in which I can partner up with other amazing people to share our brilliance and add more value to people's lives. I have never been a believer in the saying, "If it is to be, it's up to me." Too many women burn themselves out by adopting that belief. If we truly want to make a difference in the world (and a substantial income) while still having a balanced life, doesn't it make more sense to team up and multiply the impact? I do a lot of networking, and my favorite thing to do is to look for ways I can connect with other people for opportunities to share existing resources or co-create something new. This can not only be financially rewarding, but also a lot more fun! To build these relationships, you must be very clear about who you are, who you serve, and you must remove any ego you have about this being a competition. When two or more people can come together with total commitment, collaboration is a win-win-win!

Jen Du Plessis writes: Your first step in developing a collaborative relationship, if you like the person, is to determine if there is common interest in being able help each other's businesses. Period.

5 Key Questions:

- Tell me about your goals for this year. What are you trying to achieve?

- Tell me about a challenge you are facing. (Examples: My assistant just quit, I need a social media person, I need more leads, etc.) *Note: Do not solve their challenge at the initial meeting.* What have you tried so far to resolve the challenge? What has worked and what has not?

- Who would you like to be connected with to help you get more exposure in your industry and for your business?

- How would I know if someone was a good fit as a client or resource for you? *Note: If they don't know, you can follow up later.*

- What are you working on right now in your business, and how can I help? (Example: Promoting an event.)

Once you are done asking these questions, you will want to answer them as well. This will help determine if you have discovered a good complementary relationship or not.

Mel Carr writes: I'm a big believer in the power of collaboration, especially when it comes to business. I've seen firsthand how two (or more) heads are better than one when it comes to brainstorming ideas, generating new leads, and closing deals. That's why I'm such a proponent of joint ventures (JVs).

For those not familiar with the term, a joint venture is basically a business partnership between two or more individuals or companies. Each party contributes something of value to the venture, and they share in the profits (and risks) associated with it. JVs can be extremely beneficial for all parties involved, providing them with access to new markets, resources, and ideas.

I've had a lot of success with JVs over the years, both as a way to grow my business and to generate new income streams. And I know that if you're looking to take your business to the next level, JVs are definitely worth considering. Just make sure that you choose your partners carefully and clearly define everyone's roles and responsibilities from the outset. With a little planning and preparation, JVs can be extremely profitable endeavors for all businesses involved.

Shari Weller writes: Collaboration is not only fun, but also a great way to get into other people's networks. For my business, I have always used networking events to look for collaborative partners. One of the best benefits of collaboration is that it's a win-win situation. I have used collaboration to offer events, webinars, and workshops and to make friends with similar interests.

When looking for a collaborative partner, here are some things to consider:

- Look for people who serve the same demographic, but are not your competition.

- Look for people you would enjoy working with and who have a similar work ethic.

- Look for someone who has different strengths than you.

- Look for someone who can complement your business, and vice-versa.

Best Practices & Advice Around Building & Utilizing Community

Mel Carr writes: I'm a huge advocate for community over competition, and I think that's one of the key reasons why I've been so successful as a six-figure chick entrepreneur. There's just something really special about being surrounded by like-minded, ambitious women who are all working towards similar goals.

We lift each other up, we offer advice and support, and we celebrate each other's successes. I honestly don't know where I would be without my entrepreneurial girlfriends. So, if you're thinking about starting your own business or you are already running one but feeling a little isolated, my advice is to seek out a community of like-minded women. It will make all the difference in your success.

Shari Weller writes: Community has never been more vital than it is now. When the world shut down, people lost their sense of community. Now, more than ever, people want to be a part of something! Building community can not only be beneficial for building friendships, but it can also help build your business as well.

There are several different ways to either build or join a community:

- Use social media to find online communities. Become an active participant. Like and comment on posts and use DM to connect with people of interest.

- Use meetup.com to find groups with common interests.

- Attend networking events.

- If you have kids, get involved with school activities, sports, etc.

- Find a philanthropy that resonates with your goals.

- If you like going to the gym, join a fitness class.

Best Practices & Advice Around Leadership

Jennifer Drago writes: Based on my 30 years of leadership experience, I offer the following advice to any current or future leader:

- Walk in their shoes. Understand every business that you manage from the ground up. You can be a better leader and support your employees better if you have this understanding.

- Walk the talk. Nothing will distance you from your subordinates faster than a "do as I say, not as I do" stance.

- Don't expect your employees to do anything that you aren't willing to do. One way I was able to build credibility and trust with employees early in my career was to roll up my sleeves and work alongside them when they were slammed.

- Seek to understand first. If someone doesn't perform to expectations, did they understand what was expected of them? Were they properly trained? What was their intent? Otherwise, we risk alienating a good employee by jumping to the wrong conclusion.

- Get to know your team members by learning about their interests, their families, and what is important to them. Showing an interest in them will foster their trust in you.

- Be radically transparent and honest, even when the communication is unpleasant or not good news. Honesty and transparency will breed loyalty and trust.

- Give praise generously where it is due.

Best Practices & Advice Around Family

Mel Carr writes: I'm a female entrepreneur, and family is one of the keys to my success. I come from a long line of strong women; my mom and grandmother were my most significant role models. Unfortunately, my grandmother is no longer with us; however, she is watching over me! They taught me the importance of hard work, dedication, and persistence. My mom helped me get funding and cheered me on when things got tough. I'm so grateful to have her in my life, and I know her support has been instrumental to my success. So, if you're thinking about starting your own business, make sure you have a strong support system. Your family can be your biggest asset on the journey to entrepreneurship.

Best Practices & Advice Around Philanthropy

Jennifer Drago writes: As someone whose career has been primarily in the nonprofit sector and who has personally founded three nonprofits, I believe that good core values and a philanthropic mindset are foundational for business leaders. I would hope that everyone who is fortunate to have their health, a job, and a place to live would be willing and able to give back in some way to serve the needs of others. Philanthropy can be in the form of time, talent, treasure, or testimony:

- **Time:** Volunteer for your favorite cause or nonprofit. Every nonprofit needs volunteers to serve its mission. Just a few hours a month can make a world of difference.

- **Talent:** Serve as a board member for a nonprofit. Many have small staffs and need the talent and expertise of board members to guide the organization and potentially assist with some of the specialized tasks of the organization.

- **Treasure:** Donate goods, services, or dollars to a nonprofit of your choice.

- **Testimony:** When you have been touched by the nonprofit personally, or have been moved by the work that a nonprofit does, offer your testimonial (written or oral) so that the nonprofit can use it in its promotion. Your words can influence the actions of others to serve or donate to the nonprofit's mission.

Julie Jones writes: My favorite quote is, "To whom much is given, much is expected." It's a philosophy by which I have lived my life. I grew up in a middle-class family, and there were times when money was really tight.

Yet, my parents instilled in me the idea to always give back to those who may need it even more. It's an important part of my giving attitude, to be in support of others without judgment. I tithe and make charitable contributions with time and money on a set schedule. I have seen time and time again that what I give away comes back to me 100 times over.

What's Next?

You may not be thinking about what's next for you after reading this, since we've given you so many action items on which to get started... shifting your mindset, reflecting, working on your marketing, rethinking your money management, examining best practices, and so much more.

The reality is, however, that most entrepreneurs fail. Most go out of business because they don't learn how to run a consistent, moneymaking business. Most don't get or seek the help and mentorship to support them, get them where they need to go next, or tell them what to do and when.

Do YOU have an obstacle or challenge that we didn't mention, and which you aren't sure how to overcome? Do you need advice or best practices on how to tackle something in your business that we didn't talk about? Reach out to myself or to any of the authors: we can help!

The Six-Figure Chicks authors understand where you're coming from; we get you. We also understand where you want to go and some of the struggles you'll face along the way.

I recommend you reach out to a few of the authors in this book for support, guidance, and even just to congratulate them. Reaching six figures is not an easy feat. Staying there and growing even farther is tougher yet. We know how to help you navigate around the obstacles while sustaining the least amount of damage, and then take advantage of the advice so YOU can see six-figure (or more!) success in your business, too.

My goal is to help people like you create happier lives for themselves. I will do that by taking tasks off your plate that you either aren't good at, don't like to do, or don't want to do, so that they get done and you make a bigger impact and a lot more money doing what you love!

We've hired mentors to help us get where we are. Let me and some of the other authors help you get where you want to go. Trust me, you will waste time and money on the wrong things if you don't.

Don't deny yourself the success you're seeking and which you deserve.

Don't let your fears and doubts get in the way... just take it one step at a time.

You can do this!

About the Author

MEL CARR, FOUNDER & CEO OF CLOVERSY LLC. AN EXECUTIVE VIRTUAL ASSISTANT COMPANY

"I make time to listen, seek, and discover new revelations about myself and others. Open to beauty, meaning, and purpose, I look for ways to connect with what is "above and beyond" my limitations. My life is enriched by a strong measure of gratitude, humor, playfulness, and acceptance of what I can't control. I can discover fresh and startling ideas, and I am able to genuinely grapple with mystery and what is sacred in life."

- Mel Carr, Founder & CEO of Cloversy.com

Want to learn how utilizing a virtual assistant can help you scale your business to Six Figures and beyond?

Book a Private Discovery Call with Mel today!

We can help you to:

- Automate your marketing

- Book more speaking gigs

- Implement the right technology

- Manage and connect on social media

- Accelerate your brand with amazing graphics

- Maintain and uplevel an effective website

- Create effective lead generation funnels

- Build and nurture your contacts

- Enjoy more freedom in your life

- Delegate and grow your team

- And more!

Sign up today at
www.Cloversy.com/contact

Interested in Becoming One of the Authors in an Upcoming Book of Ours?

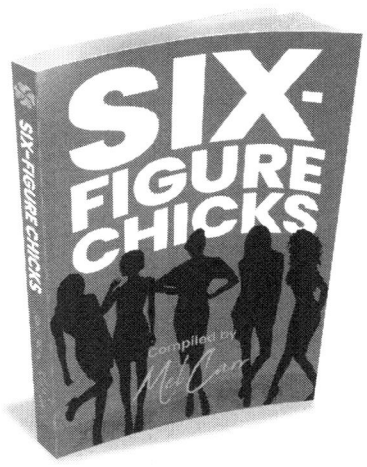

Being an author sets you apart from others in your industry and it impresses your clients! Writing one chapter in a compilation book like this one is much faster and easier than writing an entire book yourself. It's great to have your own full book, but being in a compilation book or two or three is a great place to start. Plus, all the authors share and promote the book too, giving you more visibility in many markets.

Get on our email list to be first to hear when we do this again at Cloversy.com.

Made in the USA
Middletown, DE
28 May 2024

54855392R00093